ESSENTIAL
HERBS

ESSENTIAL
HERBS

The 100 Best for Design and Cultivation

Text and Photography by Derek Fell

CRESCENT BOOKS
NEW YORK

A FRIEDMAN GROUP BOOK

This 1990 edition published by Crescent Books
distributed by Crown Publishers, Inc.
225 Park Avenue South
New York, New York 10003

LIBRARY OF CONGRESS CATALOGING-IN-PUBLICATION DATA

Fell, Derek.
    Essential herbs / by Derek Fell.
       p.   cm.
    ISBN 0-517-67882-1
    1. Herbs. 2. Herbs—Pictorial works. 3. Herb gardening. 4. Herb
gardens.   I. Title.
    SB351. H5F43   1989
    635'.7—dc20   89-27406
                                                                        CIP

ESSENTIAL HERBS: The 100 Best for Design and Cultivation
was prepared and produced by
Michael Friedman Publishing Group, Inc.
15 West 26th Street
New York, New York 10010

This book is intended as a reference only. Do not attempt to diagnose
or treat any illness without the advice of a professional. The
information presented here is not to substitute for any treatment
prescribed by a physician.

Typeset by: Mar + X Myles Graphics, Inc.
Color Separation by: United South Sea Graphic Art Co., Ltd.
Printed and bound in Hong Kong by South China Printing Co. (1988) Limited

h g f e d c b a

DEDICATION

For Linda.

ACKNOWLEDGMENTS

Thanks to the many herbalists who shared with me their gardens, especially to Cyrus Hyde, owner of Well-Sweep Herb Garden, Port Murray, New Jersey; Phyllis Schaudys, owner of Herbal Acres, Fort Washington, Pennsylvania; and the garden staff at Conestoga House, Lancaster, Pennsylvania.

TABLE OF CONTENTS

INTRODUCTION

WORTH THEIR WEIGHT IN GOLD

BOTANICALLY SPEAKING, THERE IS NO CLEAR-cut classification for "an herb." "Herb" is simply an accepted term used to describe a group of plants with useful properties. In addition to their culinary uses, herbs are sources for dyes, medicines, and insect repellents.

Some horticulturists like to define an herb as any annual, perennial, or biennial that provides useful benefits and can be grown from seed. They consider everything else that doesn't grow readily from seed, such as bulbs (saffron) and even woody plants (bay laurel tree), spices.

The terms "herbs" and "spices" are often used interchangeably, though spices normally refer to culinary powders and small fragrant pieces, such as ginger, that originate from woody plants. For example, black pepper, cinnamon, and cloves are all derived from tropical trees. It was the high value placed on these spices that inspired Christopher Columbus to seek a shorter route to the Far East, where these precious commodities grew. Although Columbus found many interesting and valuable new plants when he discovered the Americas, including potatoes, tobacco, and cocoa trees, relatively few native American plants (such as allspice, chili peppers, and bergamot) have added to the list of important herbs and spices.

There is a fine distinction between the accepted notion of a "vegetable" and that of an "herb." Most vegetables are a complete food in themselves (lettuce, tomatoes, peas), while herbs generally enhance or complement the flavor of meat, poultry, and fish, among other things. It is generally believed that the first gardens were grown as food gardens, producing essential grains and vegetables, but there is evidence to support the notion that man's first cultivated crop was an herb, probably a medicinal or hallucinogenic one. We do know herbs have a rich history. From ancient times through the nineteenth century, herbs were an essential element in civi-

Right: This classical knot garden design at Well-Sweep Herb Farm in New Jersey takes on autumnal hues following fall frosts.

Opposite page: Parallel beds of silvery lamb's ears *(Stachys olympica)* line a walkway leading to a Colonial-style outhouse at Well-Sweep Herb Farm in Port Murray, New Jersey.

lized society, helping mask unpleasant household odors before the invention of modern plumbing, and disguising and enhancing the flavor of bland or putrid foodstuffs before the advent of modern refrigeration. Prior to modern medicinal treatments, herbs were often the only form of relief known for all manner of ailments.

Merchants seeking sources of herbs—especially for spices and to use as perfumes—found them growing all over the world. Sage, for example, was found along the shores of the Mediterranean; tarragon was first discovered in Siberia; and ginger is believed to have been brought from China. Native American herbs include bergamot and sassafras, both popular flavorings for tea.

The costliest spice in the world is undoubtedly saffron, gathered from the glowing red stigmas, or female flower parts of *Crocus sativus*. In value, it is worth more than its weight in gold—an ounce currently costs more than $2,000.00! Not easy to flower, difficult to grow in colder climates, it is a commercial crop in parts of Spain and Kashmir. Harvested by hand, it requires up to 100,000 blossoms to yield one pound of dried saffron stigmas. Though a beautiful yellow dye can be made from saffron, its principal use is in flavoring Mediterranean and Oriental dishes, especially French bouillabaisse soup, Spanish paella, and Italian risotto.

English lavender is another valuable herb crop, grown mostly in the county of Norfolk, northeast of London. Unlike the shy-blooming saffron crocus, English lavender is relatively easy to grow throughout North America. It flowers for most of the summer and looks highly decorative in a flower border; it also produces one of the most cherished fragrances in the world.

Because herbs are such diverse plants, they can serve many functions in the landscape. Some, such as chamomile and thyme, can be grown as ground covers; others, such as hops and nasturtium, can be trained as vines; and still others, such as chives and foxglove, will serve well as ornamentals.

Presented here are some ideas for growing herbs in imaginative ways, including some classic herb garden designs, plus instructions for propagating herbs, lists for many varied uses, and a concise encyclopedia section describing 100 of the most useful.

CHAPTER ONE

GROWING HERBS

PROPAGATING HERBS

THE MAJORITY OF HERBS CAN BE PROPAGATED in at least one of three ways: by seed, by cuttings, and by root division. Some herbs, such as lavender and mint, are easily propagated by all three methods.

STARTING FROM SEED

For those herbs that grow easily from seed, this is the best and most inexpensive way to grow large numbers of plants. A packet of lavender seed, for example, is sufficient to grow hundreds of plants. There are three seed-starting systems to consider: direct-seeding into the garden, in which the seeds are sown where plants are to mature; the two-step method, whereby seeds are started in a peat pot or peat pellet and then transplanted into the garden; and the three-step method, whereby plants are first started in a seed tray, then transplanted into a peat or plastic pot, and then finally transferred to the garden.

Direct-Seeding generally requires reading the packet instructions to see how deeply the seeds must be sown. If the packet does not specify a planting depth, sow seeds at a depth three times the diameter of the seed. Scratch a furrow to the required depth and sow the seeds along it. Then simply cover the seed with soil, making sure to keep the seed bed moist and weed-free until seeds germinate. When the young seedlings are large enough to handle, thin them so they do not compete against each other for space. If fertile soil is called for, it is best to fertilize the bed about ten days before sowing the seeds so that the fertilizer does not "burn" the delicate seedlings.

Two-Step Seed-Starting requires peat pots and potting soil or a Jiffy-7 or Jiffy-9 peat pellet. The peat pots need to be filled with potting soil. The peat pellets do not need soil and will expand to several times their size once immersed in water. Press the seeds into the growing medium and keep the pot or pellet moist. An ideal temperature is 70°F. Allow the seeds to germinate and then thin out the seedlings in stages until just one healthy plant remains to fill the pot or pellet. When it is time to transplant, dig a hole for the pellet or pot, place the transplant into the hole, and firm the soil around it to anchor the plant in its location. For best root development, the bottom of the peat pot should be peeled away, releasing the roots; and if the pellet has a net holding it together, carefully remove it.

Three-Step Seed-Starting consists of filling a seed tray made from peat or plastic with potting soil. Scatter the seeds over the soil surface and lightly cover them—there should be enough soil on top of them to anchor the seeds. Moisten the soil and keep the tray inside a clear plastic bag until the seeds germinate. The plastic bag prevents rapid drying out of the soil and creates a humid micro-climate, ideal for germinating seeds. The optimum temperature for germination is 70°F.

When the seeds have germinated, use a sharp pencil and your forefinger to raise the seedlings out of the seed tray and into individual peat pots. Keep the pots warm and in bright light (but *not* direct sunlight) until they are large enough to tolerate transplanting into the garden. If the transplants are in individual plastic pots, try to disturb the roots as little as possible. Tender varieties may need frost protection if frost threatens; this can be done by covering over with "hot-caps" or floating on covers.

Taking Cuttings Herbs such as mint and lavender are very easy to propagate by cutting off a 4- to 6-inch stem section, making sure to include a node at the base of the cutting. Root it in a moist, sandy potting soil. Some herbs, such as mint, will root in just plain water. Others, such as lavender, will enjoy a greater success rate if the cut end is first dipped in a rooting hormone, such as Rootone, before placing the cutting in potting soil. Bury the cut end with at least one inch of soil. Batches of cuttings can be started in seed trays and the container enclosed in a clear plastic bag to create a humid micro-climate.

Multiplying by Division Many perennial herbs, including mints, sage, and chives, spread over an area and sometimes become invasive. Once established, these plants can be divided every year to keep them from becoming unruly. These divisions are an excellent source of new plants for filling in other parts of the garden, or for trading with friends. Division is best done in the fall or the spring using a sharp, heavy-duty trowel to break up clumps. Sometimes the planting is so tightly matted that a garden fork may be required to break clumps apart.

Some herbs, such as mint, root so easily from division that even a 3-inch section of root will sprout a new plant. Botanically, these are called "root cuttings." Many other herbs, such as orris root (an iris), multiply by a bulb or rhizome produced by the mother plant, and it is relatively easy to dig them up, break them apart, and replant them.

Left: An assortment of herb seedlings ready to be transplanted into the garden. Seed-starting is the most inexpensive way to grow lots of herbs.

Below: A windowsill planting of assorted herbs and leaf lettuce growing indoors during winter.

SEED-STARTING METHOD #1

1—Scatter the seeds thinly over the soil surface in a seed tray.

2—Thin out the seedlings to leave only the healthiest plants.

3—When the seedlings are large enough to handle, transfer them to individual pots.

4—Place a group of seeds in the planting hole of a peat pellet.

5—Thin the seedlings to a single, strong plant.

6—Gently remove the netting to free the roots at the time of transplanting.

SEED-STARTING METHOD #2

1—Place the seeds in individual compartments of a plastic six-pack.

2—Thin the seedlings to one per compartment.

3—Press the bottom of the flexible plastic compartment to pop out each root ball for transplanting.

SEED-STARTING METHOD #3

1—Place seeds in a fiber or a peat pot.

2—Thin to one plant per pot. Let the roots penetrate the sides.

3—Tear out the bottom of the pot prior to planting.

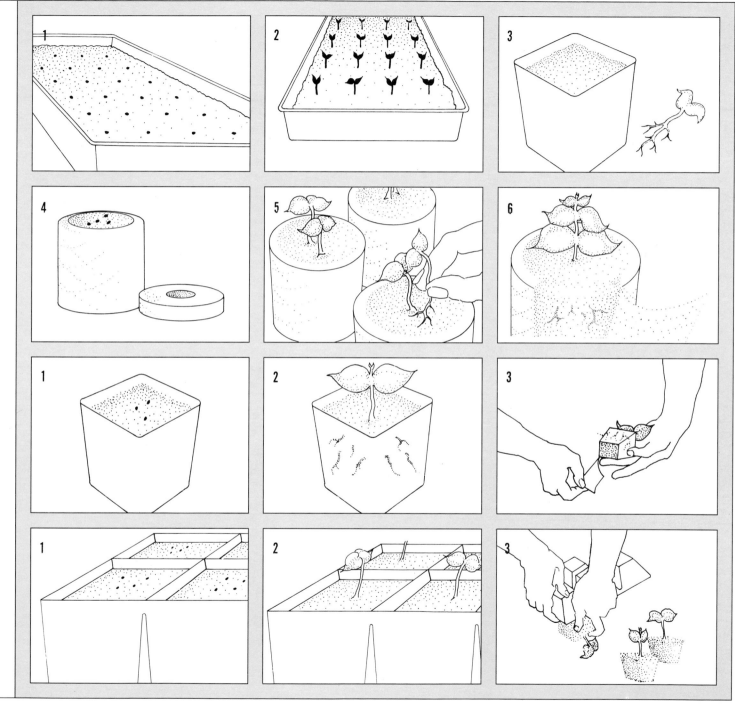

Left: Herbs and perennials are combined in these flower beds at Mt. Vernon, Virginia, the home of General George Washington.

SMALL SEEDS-STARTING METHOD #1

1—Pour the seeds directly from the packet onto a teaspoon.

2—Pick up the seeds individually with the moist end of a pencil.

3—Place the seeds in rows on a moist paper towel.

4—Roll the towel loosely. Keep it warm and moist. Most fine seeds need light to germinate.

5—Examine the towel after the required germination period.

6—Use the end of a moist pencil and forefinger to pick the seedlings off of the towel. Transfer to individual peat pots.

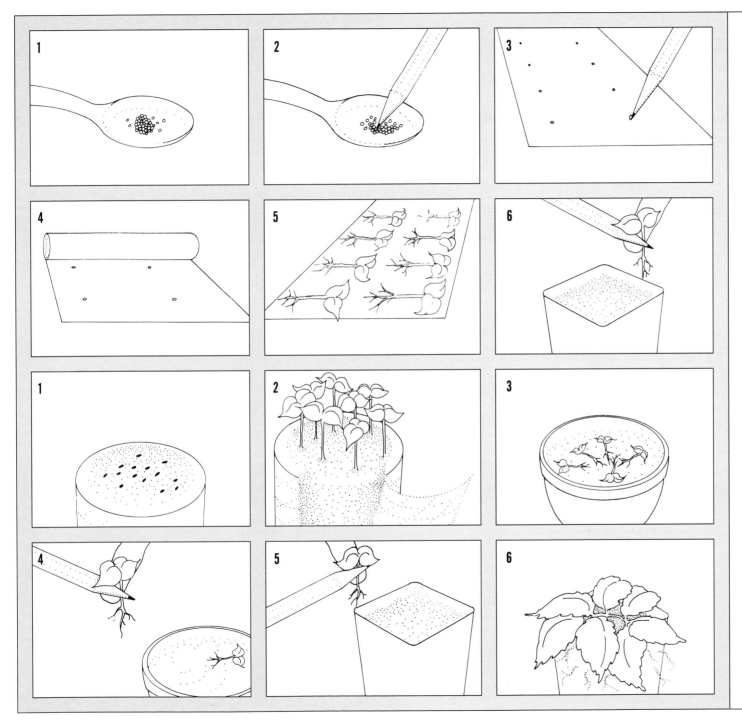

1—Sprinkle the seeds onto the surface of a peat pellet. Press seeds into surface, but do not cover. Keep moist and warm.

2—When seeds have all sprouted, tear away the pellet netting.

3—Submerge the pellet into a bowl of water. The soil and seedlings will separate. The seedlings will float.

4—Using a moist pencil point and forefinger, gently lift the seedlings individually.

5—Transfer them to individual peat pots filled with planting mix.

6—When the plants reach transplanting size, the peat pot can be planted directly into the garden to allow freedom for the roots to grow.

STEM CUTTINGS

1—Cut off a 5-inch-long side shoot.

2—Remove lower leaves.

3—Dip end in rooting hormone.

4—Set firmly in soil mix.

5 and 6—Place cuttings in a propagator made from a seed flat and cover it with plastic.

7—As an alternative, use a deep box covered with glass.

8—Set out in cold frames during the winter.

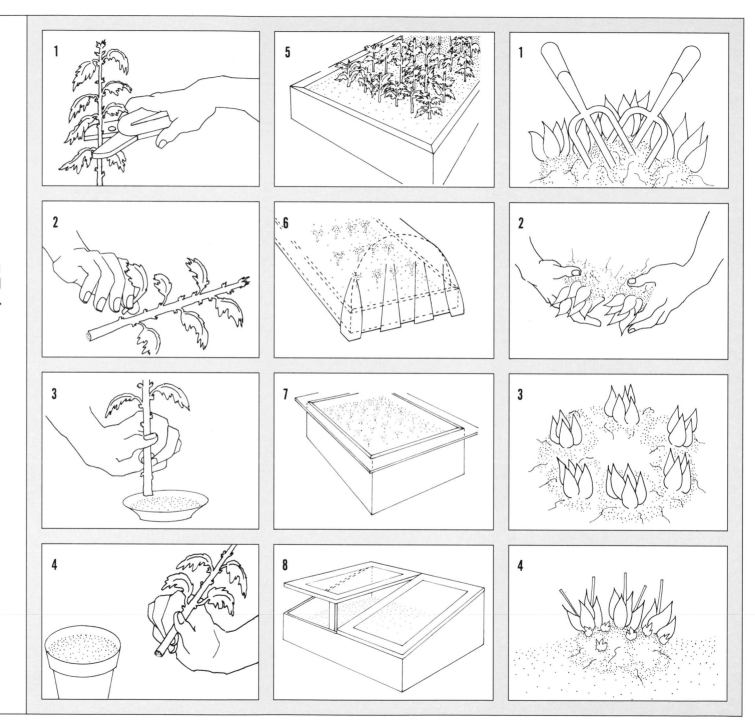

Right: The kitchen garden at the Governor's Palace in Williamsburg, Virginia features both salad greens and herbs. The white flower heads of chervil are conspicuous in the foreground.

ROOT DIVISIONS

1—Separate thick clumps into smaller clumps by using a garden fork.

2—Separate smaller clumps by hand, ensuring each clump has a healthy growing crown and roots.

3—In the ground, a typical clump will look like this— with the thick root ball hollow in the middle. Sometimes new growth is not as obvious, especially after fall frost.

4—Lift clump with fork or spade. Wash away large clumps of soil. Each new division should contain new growth or buds, old stems, and a root system.

Right: A raised planter overflows with basil and chives in this combination vegetable and herb garden designed by horticulturalist Ed Toth.
Opposite page: Here, herbs are planted in decorative pots and placed around a sundial.

GROWING HERBS IN CONTAINERS

Most herbs grow well in containers; in fact, this is often the best way to stop the aggressive kinds from being too invasive. Many herbs, particularly culinary favorites such as chives, parsley, and thyme, can be grown in small containers. They develop their pungency early, and even a 4-inch pot can accommodate a healthy clump that will be sufficient to provide a light supply of fresh seasonings. Obviously, the bigger the pot the more you can grow, and the less likelihood of having the container dry out.

Clay pots generally work best. When clean, they are not only attractive, but do not overheat as quickly as plastic containers do. Ceramic and rot-resistant wood are also good materials to use as herb containers because of their insulating ability; metal is not. In a sunny window or on a hot patio, metal can become so hot that the roots will burn.

Herbs grown in pots need a potting soil that is on the heavy side (with garden loam added) to provide good anchorage. Many peat based potting soils are too light and fluffy unless mixed with garden loam. Containerized plants—especially hanging baskets—need watering almost daily and regular amounts of fertilizer, which is best applied in a weak strength at the time of watering. Hanging baskets usually need more moisture because they are subjected to excessive air circulation.

Whatever type of pot you choose to use, it must have good drainage. Most commercial plant pots already have drainage holes punched in the bottom and some even come with a useful drainage tray to collect excess water. To stop the potting soil from falling through the drainage holes—and also to prevent them from clogging up by soil compaction—it is best to place a few pebbles or convex pieces of broken clay pots over the holes. Some commercial containers come with a device built into the bottom to keep the holes cleared, such as a raised wire platform.

Most herbs will tolerate being pot-bound, and can be kept compact by pruning, but eventually they will benefit from being transplanted into a larger pot. Salt build up from the

use of chemical fertilizers should be watched. When the soil surface is caked with salts, consider re-potting. If you live in an area with a cold climate, try growing some tender herb species that can be moved outdoors during warm weather. Lemon trees, bay laurel, ginger, and basil are examples of tender plants that can be overwintered in pots.

Another group of herb plants can be trained into interesting shapes, such as topiary, bonsai, and espalier forms. Myrtle, for example, can be grown so it has a slender, straight trunk and a rounded top. Quince makes an exquisite bonsai subject—and, even though you can dwarf the plant by restricting its roots and by pruning, the fruit will always be full size. The multiple branches of rosemary can be trained to splay out like a fan (a popular form of espalier).

Growing Herbs Indoors To grow herbs successfully indoors, they are best cultivated in containers (see above) and provided with bright light, but not direct sunlight, which can cause rapid moisture loss and "sunscorch." Try to give plants light that is not too direct. A plant placed too far back from a bright window, for example, will have a tendency to stretch and exhaust itself. A good way to ensure an even distribution of light in a window location is to purchase a window greenhouse that works like a bay window, projecting out from the house one or two feet, with several rows of shelves to grow a wide assortment of plants.

When there is a total absence of natural daylight it's possible to use grow lights. For most herbs, pairs of grow lights should be set 6 to 8 inches above the plants, under a reflector canopy. Check garden supply houses for specific brands and complete growing instructions. These fluorescent lights will enable you to grow herbs even in a dark basement. They generally need to burn sixteen hours a day for optimum growth and are best set on timers so the lights switch on and off automatically.

How to Buy Herbs There is such a great year-round demand for herbs that even discount stores may have a selection to offer, although a garden center, florist, or houseplant outlet may carry a better selection. For the best selection, however, try locating a local "herb farm." Herb farms are now a popular cottage industry, and you will find a good selection offered for sale in pots varying in size from young transplants to mature potted topiaries and hanging baskets.

Some of these herb farms do a mail-order trade and by checking the source list on page 124 you will find names of some reliable mail order herb specialists you can write to for their catalog. The success rate from mail-order herbs is quite good. Only herbs that travel safely through the mail are offered. Generally, they are shipped in small pots; the soil is prevented from shaking loose by a tight plastic wrapper. Sometimes—if the plant is shrubby—you may receive a bare-root cutting with the roots wrapped in moist sphagnum moss for protection, and occasionally you will receive dormant bulbs, as in the case of saffron crocus and orris root. When buying from mail-order sources, read the order form carefully for instructions on how to enter your order and the waiting period to expect. When plants arrive, examine the package immediately and request a replacement if there is evidence of serious damage or wilt, and plant as soon as weather conditions allow.

DESIGNING WITH HERBS

Herbs work best in the landscape when they are grown in a special area (preferably close to the kitchen) where there is a strong sense of design to the overall layout since many herbs are not sufficiently ornamental to dress up an uninspired landscape like colorful annuals and perennials. Herbs look particularly good in highly formal designs, such as parterre gardens and knot gardens, where they can be used to delineate planting beds. The "cartwheel design" in particular is a great favorite, whereby paths radiate from a center point like the spokes of a wheel, the pie-shaped areas between the spokes serving as planting beds. For blueprints of specific garden designs, see chapter 4, "Garden Plans."

Once you have a highly formal layout in place, the plantings can be extremely informal. In fact, the very best herb gardens generally combine a strong formal design with a deliberate softening of the edges accomplished with plants that spill into the pathways, create billowing cushions, or punctuate the design with tall flower spikes.

While it is possible to have an herb garden with a preponderance of flowering plants, the best herb gardens rely more heavily on creating subtle and subdued color by concentrating more on texture, form, and gradations of green, silver,

and purple—hues commonly found in their leaves. Texture comes from recognizing the beauty of leathery, shiny leaves like bay laurel, and contrasting them with the woolly, glistening leaves of lamb's ears. Form is introduced by accentuating the shapes of plants, for example exposing the strong, spreading multiple stems of a quince tree by pruning away lower side branches and ringing it with the low-growing, ground-hugging, cushionlike form of thyme or santolina.

It's possible to create theme gardens using herbs. For example, an herb garden can look "Ecclesiastical" by placing a font or other religious artifact at the center as a focal point. It can be given a "Gothic" or "Medieval" look by using low wattle fences to divide planting beds; these wattle fences are made by weaving together pliable branches.

POPULAR HERB GARDEN DESIGN THEMES:

Beehive Herb Garden: uses a beehive as a focal accent.

Biblical Herb Garden: shaped like a cross, contains plants of the Bible.

Butterfly Herb Garden: layout simulates the outstretched wings of a butterfly.

Cameo Herb Garden: herbs planted by use—dye plants together, etc.

Cartwheel Herb Garden: spaces between spokes become planting beds.

Elizabethan Herb Garden: hexagonal cartwheel design with brick paths.

Knot Garden: herbs planted as low hedges to make parterre designs.

Medieval Herb Garden: low wattle fences used as an edging to a geometric design.

Monastery Herb Garden: includes a well head as a focal accent.

POPULAR STRUCTURES FOR HERB GARDENS:

Arbors	Fonts
Benches	Gazebos
Birdbaths	Outhouses
Birdhouses	Sculpture: especially St. Fiacre,
Brick Paths	the patron saint of gardeners
Flagstones	Terra-cotta containers

A "Butterfly" herb garden can be created by introducing herbal plants, such as beebalm, that attract butterflies, and by laying out the garden in the shape of a butterfly's outstretched wings.

Another enterprising herb garden design is the "Cameo" garden, whereby herbs for special purposes are grouped together. For example, herbs with culinary qualities could be grouped in one section, insect repellent plants in another, and herbs used for perfumes in another. Another type of Cameo garden includes garden beds that represent different themes. For example, an oval space edged with a low wattle fence and a unicorn statue in the middle can represent a "medieval garden;" a bed of plants attractive to bees can feature a beehive in the middle to create a "beehive garden," and so on.

Care should be taken when designing with herbs to ensure that tall plants, such as dill, do not obscure shorter ones, such as lavender.

An especially attractive type of herb garden is the knot garden which uses dwarf herbs to create miniature hedges that can be planted in merging swirls and circles (see sample designs, pages 100 to 101). Generally, three foliage colors are used—dark green, silver, and purple—as are shrubby plants that can tolerate repeated shearing to keep the outlines sharp and well-defined. Usually, santolina is used for a silver effect, germander for the dark green, and pygmy barberry for the purple. Use different colored gravel in the geometric spaces created by the hedges.

SOIL PREPARATION

Herbs generally do not demand as rich a soil as do other garden plants, such as vegetables, flowering annuals, and perennials. Many herbs grow in the most inhospitable places—sage on rocky hillsides bordering the Mediterranean Sea, scented geraniums in the desertlike areas of South Africa, and tarragon on the bleak steppes bordering the Arctic Circle. Herbs are tough survivors that developed strong fragrances and flavors as protection against insects or foraging animals. Where soil conditions are too difficult for vegetables or ornamentals, you might succeed with selections of easy-to-grow herbs such as sage, lavender, and thyme.

In general, herbs prefer a soil pH that is slightly acidic. If you are unsure about the nature of your soil, contact your local County Extension Agent for instructions on how to take a soil sample and mail it to a soil testing laboratory for analysis. The lab will respond with a report that tells you what your soil needs to grow a particular crop.

Soil generally can be classifed as sand, clay, or loam. The particles in sandy soil do not retain moisture or nutrients.

Clay soil is thick and impervious to moisture. Rainwater will lie on the surface of clay soil for a long time. It is cold and lumpy, and sticks together in a mass when you pick up a handful and squeeze it in your hand.

Loam soil is loose and crumbly. Even when moist you can squeeze it in your hand and it will fall apart when released. Loam soil has a high humus content (decomposed organic matter) which gives the soil the ability to hold moisture like a sponge, while still allowing excess moisture to drain away.

Soils that are too light and sandy or too heavy and contain too much clay can be improved by adding organic matter to create humus. Well-decomposed animal manure, leaf mold (the product of well-decomposed leaves), garden compost, and peat are all good sources of organic matter.

To prepare a new site for planting herbs, mark out the area with string to make squares and rectangles, or coils of garden hose to make circles, ovals, or kidney shapes. Remove sod from the surface, shake it free of soil, which can be returned to the site, and discard the sod onto a compost pile. Dig the site over to a depth of 12 inches and add generous amounts of compost, even if the soil is good quality garden loam. If the site drains poorly, or has hard subsoil difficult to dig, consider laying down a foundation of broken stones or large pieces of gravel to create a raised bed. Fill it with topsoil brought from elsewhere in the garden.

If a soil test has determined that the soil is too alkaline (as in desert regions), building a raised bed with corrected soil trucked in may be preferable to correcting the existing soil through amendments. Where soil is only slightly alkaline, correction can be achieved by adding sulphur at the rate recommended by the soil analysis. Where soil is acidic, correction is generally possible by adding lime at the rate recommended by the soil test.

CHAPTER TWO

USING HERBS

HERBS CAN BE USED FRESH, DRIED, OR BOTH. The time of harvesting depends on the individual herb and the use to be made of it. For example, parsley and chives are prized for fresh use and pieces of leaf as a garnish can be harvested at any time, providing plants are not weakened by over-picking. Usually, for fresh use, the younger leaves on the plant provide the best flavor. With mint, for example, the first whorl of leaves (no lower than the first six leaves from the tip) provides the best flavor.

Many herbs cannot be used instantly; they must be left to mature. Either the flowering part (as with lavender) or the root (as with ginseng) is valued, so patience is needed until a particular plant part is ready for harvest (usually one growing season in the case of lavender, but as much as three years in the case of ginseng). The individual descriptions in the encyclopedia section of this book (beginning on page 33) provide specific information on each herb.

USING FRESH HERBS

When an herb is to be used fresh for culinary purposes (such as adding to a salad, flavoring a soup, or making a refreshing tea) it should be picked just prior to use; once picked, never leave it in the sun for any length of time, or deprive it of water so it wilts. If there might be any delay between the time the herb is picked and the time it is used, just pop the stems in a jar of water. Herbs such as watercress, mint, parsley, and basil will even look decorative sitting in a jar on a kitchen windowsill until ready to be used.

DRYING HERBS

Generally, herbs are dried for two reasons: to preserve the herb for storage until you are ready to use it, or to preserve the herb for decoration, generally for use in potpourri and wreaths. Many herbs dried for culinary use (such as sage, rosemary, bay, and thyme) retain their flavors a long time and can be stored in jars. When choosing herbs to dry for wreaths and potpourri we generally like to retain as much fragrance and color as possible. In both cases the method of drying is extremely important.

Methods of Drying Herbs

Drying methods depend on whether you are drying short-stemmed or long-stemmed herbs. Usually, short-stemmed herbs must be dried over screens so air circulates freely. Herbs can be dried indoors or outdoors providing they are kept out of direct sunlight. Long-stemmed herbs are best gathered into small bunches of a dozen stems each, held together by twist-ties or elastic bands, and suspended upside down from a rafter or a clothesline.

Where the intention is to harvest seeds (such as anise and caraway), the seed heads are best gathered when the seeds are ripe. Once ripe, the seed head is shaken over newspaper pages to catch the seeds as they fall. A curing period of about seven days on the newspaper is needed to reduce the moisture content for long storage. To speed up this drying process, the seeds can be placed on pie trays or cookie sheets and left in the back of a car with the windows down. Sun shining through the windows will heat up the car quickly and cure the seeds in a day. After drying the seeds, any chaff should be carefully separated out and the seeds stored in air-tight containers.

Long-stemmed herbs can be highly ornamental while they

are in the process of being dried. A good place to dry them is in a kitchen or around a fireplace. Bunches of blue lavender, red chili peppers, yellow yarrow, and silvery artemisia can not only provide an uplifting sight when visitors enter the room, but also fill the air with pleasant aromas. Even if you never find the time to chop the dried leaves and store them in jars for future use, the sheer visual delight that is a part of drying herbs is reason enough to grow and harvest them.

WAYS TO USE HERBS

Most people are familiar with the culinary uses of herbs. Usually, very small amounts of a particular herb are needed to enhance the flavor of any dish. Mint sauce is to lamb what applesauce is to pork; saffron is a vital ingredient in the preparation of the famous French soup, *bouillabaisse*, and many people feel that dill is indispensable in fish dishes. Similarly, with beverages, herbs are used as flavor enhancers. Ginger is a prime ingredient in ginger ale and ginger beer; woodruff is synonymous with May wine, and mint enlivens the taste of ice tea. Following are a few familiar and not-so-familiar ways to use herbs around the house.

Herb Teas

Some of the best herbal teas are chamomile, mint, lavender, and lemon verbena. Many herb teas are claimed to have therapeutic properties—such as calming a nervous stomach, improving digestion, and sharpening the senses—but even without those benefits they just taste good. The method for brewing herbal teas is very easy—simply place a few sprigs of the herb in a teapot and pour in boiling water. Allow the herb to steep for two minutes; pour into cups through a strainer and serve with a dash of sugar, if desired. Herbs to make teas can be used fresh or dried.

Herb Vinegars

Though herbs can be used fresh or dried to flavor vinegar, fresh herbs are best. Some of the finest herbs to use include tarragon, rosemary, and fennel. The best vinegars to use are cider vinegar, and white- and red wine vinegars purchased in gallon containers.

To make herb vinegar, insert a few sprigs of the particular herb into a glass bottle, then pour the vinegar into it so the sprigs float in the liquid. The amount of herb used depends on how strong a flavor you want. Herbal vinegars are great gifts if you use fancy glass bottles with corks as stoppers.

Herb Butters

Herb butters taste so much better than plain butter that they can almost become addictive. Particularly good herbs to consider include parsley, tarragon, chives and basil—fresh or dried, though fresh herbs are preferred, and more colorful.

To make herb butter simply take a stick (one-quarter pound) of butter and place it in a bowl. Chop the herb leaves very fine into small pieces and mix the two together by hand or with an electric beater. Pat into molds or scoop into balls and refrigerate for several hours to allow the flavor to permeate.

Candied Herbs

The flowers, petals, and leaves of certain herbs are good to candy. These include violet flowers, rose petals, and scented geranium leaves. They are mostly used to decorate cakes, cookies, and desserts. Pick only firm, blemish-free blossoms and leaves to be candied.

To candy herbs, follow this procedure: Wash the herbs and pat them dry with a paper towel. Beat one egg white until it is foamy. Hold the leaf or flower in one hand and, using a camel hair brush, gently dab it all over with the egg white. Make sure you push the brush into all the nooks and crannies above and under the flower or leaf surface. Then, sprinkle it with superfine granulated sugar. To enhance the flower color you may wish to use colored sugar (for example, blue on violets, pink on rose petals) by adding a little food coloring to the sugar. Place the flowers or leaves on waxed paper and leave them to dry for two days. Then store in tight, dry containers in layers, with a piece of wax paper separating each layer.

Herb Potpourri

The word "potpourri" is derived from the French word *pourir*, meaning to rot, since highly fragrant, long-lasting herbal mixes were made by infusing semi-dried herbs with alcohol, such as brandy. Today, however, the easiest method for making potpourri is the dry method, allowing the aromatic leaves and petals of herbs to dry thoroughly, and mixing them into a bowl. Usually, the best potpourri allow a particular herbal fragrance to dominate—for example, the aroma given off by the petals of a rose, a lemony aroma achieved by drying lemon grass and lemon verbena, or a pineapple aroma achieved through the use of pineapple sage and pineapple-scented geraniums. To help the potpourri retain its aroma for an extended period of time, it's best to mix an essential oil (such as oil of violet or oil of lavender) with a fixative (such as powdered orris root) and blend it with the dried herbal ingredients.

For the strongest aroma, store the mixture in a tight container and place it in a dark closet for about six weeks to allow the ingredients to mingle their fragrances and mature. Then, the potpourri mixture can be transferred to a decorative bowl, emptied into an attractive spice jar, or stuffed into pillows and sachets.

CHAPTER THREE

THE ENCYCLOPEDIA OF ESSENTIAL HERBS

THE FOLLOWING LISTING OF 100 POPULAR herbs is arranged alphabetically by Latin name. If you only know the common name of a plant and want to find its listing, simply check in the cross reference of botanical and common names at the back of the book (page 126) and it will refer to the page number where the common name can be found.

For all entries, heights given are average, and under certain conditions, such as high rainfall and high soil fertility, herbs may grow taller than suggested. Under "Uses," the listing will give not only the culinary use, if the herb is known for one, but also whether the herb is used for a dye, for insect repellent, for fragrance in potpourri, and any other significant use. Where a therapeutic remedy is given—such as "clearing the sinuses" in the case of mint leaves, and "aiding the digestion" in the case of anise seeds—these claims are made on the basis of common knowledge or widely accepted herbal literature. Where herbs are recommended for making tea, these should be imbibed in small amounts only, as modern medical research is finding that overdoses of certain herbs can be harmful.

No medical claims are made for any herbs in this book. Where a medical use is given, as in the case of foxglove (*Digitalis purpurea*), the use of that herb should be only in the form of a prescription and under a physician's supervision. Such herbs are recommended only for their ornamental or historical value.

BOTANICAL NAME *Achillea filipendulina*

COMMON NAME Yarrow

HEIGHT 4 to 5 feet; upright habit.

CULTURE Hardy perennial. Propagated from seed and division. Tolerates poor soil when it is in full sun. After the third year, plants generally need dividing each year to keep the clumps from becoming unruly.

DESCRIPTION Fernlike green leaves are highly aromatic when touched. Beautiful, bright yellow flower clusters appear on top of the plants in early summer. To encourage continuous bloom, remove the faded flowers.

USES Mostly grown for its dried flowers that are used to decorate herbal wreaths. Its flowers also produce a natural yellow dye. The dried flower heads, steeped in boiling water, make a refreshing tea said to aid in digestion.

BOTANICAL NAME *Agastache foeniculum*

COMMON NAME Anise Hyssop

HEIGHT 3 to 4 feet; clump-forming, shrubby habit.

CULTURE Hardy perennial. Propagated mostly from seed. Thrives in fertile loam soil and full sun, but tolerates partial shade.

DESCRIPTION Aromatic, erect plants have round, gray-green leaves and prominent spikes studded with purple flowers, similar to lavender. All plant parts are anise scented.

USES Leaves mostly used air-dried in teas and potpourri, but can be used fresh to flavor drinks and fruit salads, or as a substitute for authentic anise seed by steeping in water, then using the liquid in cakes, muffins, and cookies.

BOTANICAL NAME *Agave americana*

COMMON NAME Century Plant; American Aloe

HEIGHT Up to 5 feet, taller when flowering; rosette-forming habit.

CULTURE Tender perennial succulent plant mostly grown in pots so can be taken indoors during freezing weather. Propagated by division. Demands excellent drainage, sunny location. Tolerates poor soil and drought.

DESCRIPTION Thick, triangular, pointed blue-green leaves, with spines along the edges, emerge from a basal crown. At maturity (sometimes 100 years), a flower spike resembling an asparagus spear will emerge, opening out to reveal greenish yellow flowers attractive to hummingbirds. After flowering, plant dies but leaves "pups" or offsets around the base which will continue to grow.

USES Leaves used medicinally by Indians of the Southwestern United States. Also a modern source of steroids.

BOTANICAL NAME *Agrimonia eupatoria*

COMMON NAME Agrimony

HEIGHT 2 to 3 feet; wide, spreading habit.

CULTURE Hardy perennial. Propagated by seed and cuttings. Prefers partial shade in dry, well-drained soil.

DESCRIPTION Leaves and stalks are deep green and downy, with slender spikes of yellow flowers. All plant parts are slightly aromatic, with the flowers emitting an apricot-like spicy scent.

USES After drying, the stems, leaves, and flowers can be used to make tea. The whole plant is also used to make a yellow dye.

BOTANICAL NAME *Alchemilla vulgaris*

COMMON NAME Lady's-mantle

HEIGHT 18 inches; spreading habit.

CULTURE Hardy perennial. Propagated by division of roots and by seed. Trouble-free plant. Easy to grow in any well-drained loam soil in sun or partial shade.

DESCRIPTION Clusters of small yellow-green flowers appear on fuzzy stalks. Velvety, scalloped, fan-shaped leaves are pleated into soft folds, reminiscent of a "lady's mantle." Highly ornamental, especially as the leaves have a tendency to collect drops of dew that glisten in the light.

USES Similar to salad burnet (*Poterium sanguisorba*) in its medicinal qualities. The herb is astringent. Thought to promote drowsiness if placed under a pillow.

BOTANICAL NAME *Allium cepa proliferum*

COMMON NAME Egyptian Top Onion

HEIGHT 3 feet; erect, clump-forming habit.

CULTURE Perennial bulb propagated mostly from bulblets that form on top of pungent, hollow, onionlike stalks. Plants are extremely hardy, and multiply by forming bulblets in the soil.

DESCRIPTION Clusters of bulbs sprout slender, pointed onion-like leaves and a hollow stem topped by a cluster of inconspicuous white flowers that quickly turn into groups of three to five bulbs.

USES Both the bulbs in the soil, and the bulblets that form on the flowering stems are edible, mostly grated to substitute for onions as a seasoning in soups, sandwiches, and salads.

BOTANICAL NAME *Allium fistulosum*

COMMON NAME Welsh Onion

HEIGHT 2 to 3 feet; upright, clump-forming habit.

CULTURE Hardy perennial bulb. Propagated mostly from the seeds that follow the flowering in the second season of growth. Also propagated by division of underground bulbs. Prefers moist, fertile loam soil in full sun or partial shade.

DESCRIPTION Rounded white flower clusters are borne on hollow green stems with new leaves forming at the base of the plant.

USES Young leaves are chopped into rings and used as a garnish like chives. The bulbs are used in cooking.

BOTANICAL NAME *Allium schoenoprasum*

COMMON NAME Chive

HEIGHT 12 to 18 inches; clump-forming habit.

CULTURE Hardy perennial bulb. Propagated by seed and by dividing established clumps. Easy to grow in any well-drained loam soil in full sun or partial shade.

DESCRIPTION Rounded pink or purple flowers appear on top of slender stalks above clumps of arching, hollow, pointed leaves. Both leaves and flowers emit a mild onion flavor.

USES Leaves are chopped and used fresh, frozen, or dried as a garnish in cooking and on salads. Highly ornamental, and popular to use as an edging.

BOTANICAL NAME *Allium tuberosum*

COMMON NAME Chinese Chive; Garlic Chive

HEIGHT 2 feet; upright, clump-forming habit.

CULTURE Hardy perennial bulb. Propagated by seed and by dividing established clumps. Easy to grow in any well-drained loam soil, in full sun or partial shade.

DESCRIPTION Vigorous plants produce spikey leaves and masses of showy, white, rounded blossoms. The flowers are sweetly scented, while the leaves and bulb have a garlic odor. Highly ornamental when in bloom.

USES Leaves are snipped into salads, soups, and sauces. The dried, green seed head makes an excellent garlic vinegar. Good to use as a ground cover for erosion control on banks. Blooms midsummer.

BOTANICAL NAME *Aloe barbadensis* (formerly *Aloe vera*)

COMMON NAME Healing Plant; Barbados Aloe

HEIGHT 1 foot usually, 2 feet when flowering; rosette-forming habit.

CULTURE Tender perennial. Propagated from seed or from young side-shoots called "pups." May be grown outdoors year-round only in frost-free areas. Prefers well-drained loam or sandy soil. In northern states, popular as a houseplant grown in pots on a sunny windowsill.

DESCRIPTION White-freckled, succulent leaves have spiny edges that are broad at the base and taper to a point. Well-established plants will develop spikes of yellow flowers.

USES A moist gel on the inside of the leaves is used to relieve the pain of burns, including sunburn. Also used as a skin moisturizer and in cosmetics—especially shampoo and soaps.

BOTANICAL NAME *Aloysia triphylla*

COMMON NAME Lemon Verbena

HEIGHT 2 to 10 feet; bushy habit.

CULTURE Tender perennial becoming woody with age. Propagated mainly by root division and stem cuttings. Grown outdoors as a shrub in frost-free areas; otherwise plants are overwintered by growing in pots and taking them indoors. Prefers fertile, moist loam soil in sun or partial shade.

DESCRIPTION Inconspicuous panicles of pale lavender blossoms appear along the stems in summer. Green, heavily veined leaves are pointed, with scalloped edges. The leaves are highly fragrant, releasing a pleasant, clean, lemon scent when bruised.

USES Dried leaves retain their delightful scent for years and are used in teas, also potpourri. The extracted oil is prized for its scent and is often used in perfumery.

BOTANICAL NAME *Amaranthus hybridus hypochondriacus*

COMMON NAME Prince's-feather; Green Amaranth

HEIGHT Up to 5 feet; erect habit.

CULTURE Tender annual. Propagated by seed. Prefers fertile loam soil with plenty of organic matter, in full sun.

DESCRIPTION Deep crimson flowers are densely packed on erect spikes. Veined, pointed leaves have purple undersides. Highly ornamental when in flower.

USES Both the seeds and the leaves are edible, the seeds as a grain and the leaves as a spinach substitute. Also, the dried flower heads are popular for floral arrangements.

BOTANICAL NAME *Amorpha fruticosa angustifolia*

COMMON NAME Indigo Bush; Bastard Indigo

HEIGHT 6 to 20 feet, with 5 to 15 feet spread; shrub or tree-like.

CULTURE Hardy deciduous shrub. Tolerates poor soil, including dry, sandy soil, in full sun. Best pruned in winter or early spring to discourage a leggy, untidy appearance.

DESCRIPTION Spikes of small, purplish blue flowers bloom June through July. Small, bright green leaves in summer turn yellow in autumn. Hardy in zones 4 to 9.

USES Source of dye. Good landscape plant for poor soils where few other ornamentals will grow.

RELATED SPECIES *Amorpha nana*, known as 'Fragrant False Indigo,' grows just 3 feet high and is cultivated for its spicy fragrance.

BOTANICAL NAME *Anethum graveolens*

COMMON NAME Dill

HEIGHT 3 to 4 feet; upright habit.

CULTURE Hardy annual. Propagated by seed. Prefers moist, fertile, acid soil in full sun.

DESCRIPTION Flowers are yellow in broad, flat umbels. The aromatic seeds are flattened with a conspicuous rib. Leaves are narrow, fern-like, blue-green.

USES All parts of the plant are aromatic. The leaves and seeds in particular are used for flavoring pickles, sauerkraut, and beets. The feathery leaves are most often used to flavor fish dishes.

BOTANICAL NAME *Angelica archangelica*

COMMON NAME Angelica

HEIGHT Up to 6 feet tall, 3 feet wide; clump-forming habit.

CULTURE Hardy biennial which produces foliage the first year and flowers the second. Propagated from seed. Prefers cool, moist, alkaline soils, in sun or partial shade.

DESCRIPTION Spectacular clusters of yellow-green flowers bloom in summer. Dark green leaves are 2 to 3 feet long, with toothed edges, borne on hollow stems that are purplish at the base. All plant parts are fragrant.

USES The entire plant—finely chopped—is used mainly as a garnish with rhubarb, salads, fish, and poultry. Tea made from the root is supposed to be a tonic and stimulant. Oils are extracted from the seeds for use as a perfume fragrance and for flavoring.

BOTANICAL NAME *Anthemis nobilis* (see also *Chamaemelum nobilis*)

COMMON NAME Chamomile

HEIGHT 6 to 12 inches; low, mat-forming habit.

CULTURE Evergreen hardy perennial. Propagated by seed and by division of established clumps. Easy to grow in well-drained loam soils in full sun.

DESCRIPTION Small, yellow, buttonlike blossoms appear in summer. Leaves are light green and segmented. All parts are highly fragrant.

USES Flowers can be used fresh or dried in tea, reputed to have a calming effect on the senses.

RELATED SPECIES *Matricaria recutita*, the 'Pineapple Weed,' and other species of *Matricaria* and *Anthemis*, possess a similar fragrance and are also referred to as chamomile.

BOTANICAL NAME *Anthemis tinctoria*

COMMON NAME Golden Marguerite

HEIGHT 2½ feet; bushy, mounded habit.

CULTURE Hardy perennial. Propagated by seed and division. Prefers sandy, fertile soil in full sun.

DESCRIPTION Daisylike, golden yellow flowers are borne in profusion on erect stems in early summer. Leaves are indented, aromatic.

USES The yellow disc flowers produce a natural yellow dye. Plants are highly ornamental.

BOTANICAL NAME *Anthriscus cerefolium*

COMMON NAME Chervil

HEIGHT 2 to 3 feet; erect, clump-forming habit.

CULTURE Hardy annual. Propagated from seed. Prefers moist, fertile, loam soil in full sun.

DESCRIPTION Dainty white flower clusters appear on thin, brittle stems in summer. Leaves are bright green and resemble parsley. Flavor is sweet and mild, with a hint of anise.

USES Young leaves can be used fresh, dried, or frozen as a garnish, especially on fish and fruit salads. It is an essential ingredient in bearnaise sauce and in the "Fines Herbs" mixture of chives, plus marjoram or tarragon. Also used on salads, in soups and marinades, and combined with butter for a chicken or fish baste.

BOTANICAL NAME *Armoracia rusticana*

COMMON NAME Horseradish

HEIGHT 2 to 3 feet; clump-forming, upright habit.

CULTURE Hardy perennial. Propagated from root cuttings in spring. Prefers fertile, well-drained loam soil in full sun.

DESCRIPTION Large, dark green paddle-shaped leaves, with wavy edges, rise erect from deep, thick taproots. Small, white flowers appear in clusters among the leaves. Best confined to a special corner, otherwise plants can become invasive.

USES The white taproots are uprooted from the soil, washed clean, and dried to release the hot, pungent aroma that flavors condiments and sauces for beef, pork, and seafood.

BOTANICAL NAME *Artemisia absinthium*

COMMON NAME Wormwood

HEIGHT 4 to 5 feet; erect, clump-forming habit.

CULTURE Hardy perennial becoming woody with age. Propagated by seed, by division of established clumps, and by cuttings. Thrives in clay soils and tolerates drought. Prefers full sun. Can become leggy and untidy if not trimmed back in spring. Best divided every two to three years to encourage vigorous new growth.

DESCRIPTION Leaves are its most ornamental feature—silvery gray in appearance, slender and fuzzy. Inconspicuous yellow flowers appear in midsummer.

USES The aperitif, absinthe, was made from this plant. Also used as a main ingredient in Vermouth. Ingestion of excessive amounts is believed to cause brain damage. Diluted wormwood tea is thought to stimulate the appetite. The dried herb is popular as a moth repellent.

BOTANICAL NAME *Artemisia dracunculus sativa*

COMMON NAME French Tarragon

HEIGHT 2 to 3 feet; erect, clump-forming habit.

CULTURE Hardy perennial. Propagated by division or cuttings. There is a related variety, *Artemisia dracunculus inodora* ('Russian Tarragon'), that can be grown from seeds, but it is inferior in quality to the true French Tarragon, which is sterile. Prefers fertile, well-drained loam soil in full sun or partial shade. Plants need dividing every three years to maintain vigor.

DESCRIPTION Narrow, anise-flavored shiny green leaves are willow-like. Inconspicuous greenish white blooms are produced sporadically.

USES Essential culinary herb used to flavor vinegar and also to season spinach, mushrooms, chicken, beef, or fish.

BOTANICAL NAME *Asclepias tuberosa*

COMMON NAME Butterfly Milkweed

HEIGHT 3 feet; upright, clump-forming habit.

CULTURE Hardy perennial. Propagated by seed and division. Prefers moist, fertile loam soil in full sun.

DESCRIPTION Beautiful bright orange flower clusters are borne on stiff stems. Dark green leaves are spear-shaped. In autumn, large cradle-shaped seed pods burst to dispense fluffy air-borne seeds.

USES The orange flowers—which are highly ornamental—yield a pale yellow natural dye. The soft stem fibers are used in textiles.

BOTANICAL NAME *Baptisia australis*

COMMON NAME False Indigo; Blue Wild Indigo

HEIGHT 3 to 4 feet; bushy, clump-forming habit.

CULTURE Hardy perennial. Propagated by seed and cuttings. Tolerates a wide variety of soils, including dry or stony, in sun or partial shade.

DESCRIPTION Lupinelike flower spikes are a beautiful indigo-blue, appearing in spring. Gray-green cloverlike leaves create an ornamental effect. Attractive black pods decorate the plant in autumn and winter.

USES The seed pods are used in dried arrangements. Good cut flower; popular landscape plant for perennial borders.

BOTANICAL NAME *Borago officinalis*

COMMON NAME Borage

HEIGHT 2 to 3 feet; sprawling habit.

CULTURE Tender annual. Propagated by seed. Re-seeds itself readily. Easy to grow in most well-drained loam soils in full sun.

DESCRIPTION Pretty bicolored flowers (pink and blue) are star-shaped, borne on velvety blue-green succulent stems. Highly ornamental.

USES Borage has a cooling effect in fruit punches and wine drinks. Its leaves and flowers have a distinct cucumber flavor. Can be substituted for cucumbers in salads and drinks. Before using scrape the fresh leaves free of hairs. This also helps release the flavor. The flowers are used to decorate cakes.

BOTANICAL NAME *Calendula officinalis*

COMMON NAME Pot-marigold

HEIGHT 18 inches; mounded habit.

CULTURE Hardy annual. Propagated by seeds that can be sown where they are to bloom. Easy to grow in a wide range of soils in full sun or partial shade. Re-seeds itself readily.

DESCRIPTION Orange, yellow, or apricot-colored daisylike flowers are 3 inches across, produced continuously throughout the growing season, but most prolifically in cool weather during spring and autumn. Leaves are dark green, lancelike, soft to touch.

USES Both flowers and leaves are edible. Although bitter, small amounts can be added to soups and salads as a flavor enhancer. A yellow dye is extracted from the flowers. Highly ornamental, frequently used as a bedding plant in annual flower gardens.

BOTANICAL NAME *Camasia esculenta*

COMMON NAME Quamash

HEIGHT 1 1/2 to 2 feet; upright, spirelike habit.

CULTURE Hardy perennial bulb. Propagated from bulblets dug from the soil. Prefers acid soil in full sun.

DESCRIPTION Light blue to deep blue flower spikes are produced on poker-straight stalks. Basal lilylike leaves wither and die soon after flowering. Grows wild in open woods and meadows, especially prolific in the Pacific Northwest of the United States.

USES Once a food staple of American Indians who baked the bulbs for eating. Taste is similar to sweet potatoes.

BOTANICAL NAME *Capsicum annum*

COMMON NAME Hot Pepper; Chili Pepper

HEIGHT 1 to 2 feet; compact, bushy habit.

CULTURE Tender annual. Propagated from seed, first started indoors and then transplanted to the garden after all danger of frost has passed. Prefers a fertile loam soil high in calcium, in full sun.

DESCRIPTION Small, white, starlike flowers cover the plants in summer, produce showy, curved, pointed fruits that change color from green to bright red when fully ripe.

USES Valued in cooking for adding a fiery, hot flavor to soups, stews, and many ethnic dishes such as Indian curries and Mexican salsas. Good to grow in containers.

BOTANICAL NAME *Carthamus tinctorius*

COMMON NAME Safflower

HEIGHT 3 feet; erect, branching habit.

CULTURE Tender annual. Propagated from seed. Tolerates a wide range of soils, including impoverished, dry soil, in full sun.

DESCRIPTION Bright orange thistlelike flowers appear in summer. Indented, shiny green leaves are covered in spines.

USES The white seeds are harvested commercially to make safflower oil for cooking. Seeds are frequently incorporated into wild bird foods. The dried petals are used to color food, and can be substituted for saffron powder in a variety of dishes. The petals also yield a natural dye for cloth.

BOTANICAL NAME *Carum carvi*

COMMON NAME Caraway

HEIGHT 3 feet; feathery habit.

CULTURE Hardy biennial. Seed should be sown directly into the garden, since seedlings do not take to transplanting. Seed sown in fall bears flowers and edible seeds the following summer. Spring-sown plants bear the second year. Prefers moist, fertile, loam soil in full sun. Roots need mulching to protect them from freezing.

DESCRIPTION The finely cut leaves resemble carrot tops. White flower umbels appear in midsummer, followed by gray-brown seeds.

USES The seeds are pleasantly aromatic and popular to flavor vegetable soups, meat stews, sauerkraut, coleslaw, and fish casseroles. The oil from caraway seeds is used to flavor many liqueurs.

BOTANICAL NAME *Catharanthus roseus*

COMMON NAME Madagascar Periwinkle; Annual Vinca

HEIGHT 9 inches; low, spreading habit.

CULTURE Tender annual. Seed should be started indoors and transplanted into the garden after danger of frost has passed. Plant in full sun. Tolerates a wide range of soil conditions. Pollution resistant. Thrives in high heat.

DESCRIPTION Glossy, oval, dark green leaves form a dense ground cover. Cheerful white, pink, or purple star-shaped flowers are borne in profusion all summer.

USES The leaves contain a chemical beneficial in the treatment of Hodgkin's disease, leukemia, and other diseases. Plants are highly ornamental, suitable for containers and hanging baskets in addition to low beds and borders.

BOTANICAL NAME *Chamaemelum nobile*

COMMON NAME True Chamomile; Roman Chamomile

HEIGHT 1 inch; low, spreading, carpetlike habit.

CULTURE Hardy perennial that remains evergreen in winter except under severe conditions. Propagated from seed and division. Prefers a well-drained, sandy or loam soil in full sun. Difficult to maintain except in cool coastal areas.

DESCRIPTION There are many "false" chamomiles, including *Anthemis tinctoria* ('Golden Marguerite') and *Matricaria recutata* ('German chamomile'). The true chamomile is a much lower-growing plant, rarely exceeding 1 inch high, covering the ground like moss with tiny, green, slender leaves. Small, yellow, buttonlike flowers occur in summer. The entire plant is aromatic, and walking on it not only releases the apple-scented fragrance, it seems to stimulate the plant to grow thicker.

USES Prized for planting between flagstones, especially close to a bench where people can sit and appreciate the uplifting aroma of its bruised leaves. The flowers can be harvested and dried to make a refreshing tea.

BOTANICAL NAME *Chenopodium bonus-henricus*

COMMON NAME Good-King-Henry Goosefoot

HEIGHT 1½ to 2 feet; clump-forming habit.

CULTURE Hardy perennial. Propagated from seed. Prefers fertile loam soil in full sun.

DESCRIPTION Upper surface of the spear-shaped leaves are dark green with a lighter, slightly downy underside. Insignificant green flowers appear in spring.

USES Young leaves are harvested and cooked like spinach.

BOTANICAL NAME *Chrysanthemum balsamita*

COMMON NAME Costmary; Bible Leaf

HEIGHT 2 to 3 feet; upright, clump-forming habit.

CULTURE Hardy perennial. Propagated by root cuttings. Prefers fertile loam soil in sun or partial shade. Plant dies out in the middle after several years. Top-dressing soil with compost helps keep plants looking attractive.

DESCRIPTION Grown for its minted-scented leaves and flowers. Blossoms resemble pale yellow buttons on leggy stems that are best removed to keep plants looking attractive. The leaves are oblong and pointed with serrated edges.

USES The young leaves are used fresh or dried as a substitute for mint. Small quantities can be sprinkled on salads, also to flavor soups, poultry, and bread. The common name Bible Leaf refers to the custom among early settlers to use the dried, leathery leaves as page markers in the Bible.

BOTANICAL NAME *Chrysanthemum coccineum*

COMMON NAME Pyrethrum; Painted Daisy

HEIGHT 2 to 3 feet; bushy habit.

CULTURE Hardy perennial. Propagated from seed. Easy to grow in most well-drained loam soils in full sun. After flowering in late spring, stems can be cut back to the soil line to encourage a second flush of flowers as cool weather returns in autumn.

DESCRIPTION Beautiful daisylike flowers have yellow centers, with outer petals colored red, pink, and white. Highly ornamental. Leaves are silvery green, feathery.

USES Powdered petals are a source of an effective natural insecticide. Beautiful landscape plant for the perennial border and cutting garden.

BOTANICAL NAME *Chrysanthemum parthenium*

COMMON NAME Feverfew

HEIGHT 2 to 3 feet; bushy habit.

CULTURE Hardy perennial. Propagated by seed. Self-sows readily. Easy to grow in any well-drained loam or sandy soil in full sun.

DESCRIPTION White, cream, or yellow buttonlike flowers bloom in summer, are borne in dense clusters. Fragrant dark green leaves are soft-textured and serrated.

USES A tea brewed from the leaves was once considered a relief from headaches. Its scent is an effective insect repellent. Good to dry for winter bouquets and potpourri. Popular as a fresh cut flower.

BOTANICAL NAME *Cichorium intybus*

COMMON NAME Chicory

HEIGHT 2 to 3 feet; upright, branching habit.

CULTURE Hardy perennial. Propagated from seed. Prefers a deep, fertile loam soil in full sun.

DESCRIPTION Cheerful light blue bossoms are produced on sparse plants that are mostly stems with a few wavy green leaves. Native to Europe, plants have escaped to the wild and have become a common wayside weed.

USES Medicinally, the blue flowers were at one time distilled to make soothing eye drops. The young leaves are edible as a salad green. Also, the root can be ground to make a flavoring for coffee.

RELATED SPECIES *Cichorium endivia*, also known as 'Escarole' or 'Endive,' a high-quality salad green.

BOTANICAL NAME *Coriandrum sativum*

COMMON NAME Coriander; Chinese Parsley; Cilantro

HEIGHT 1½ to 3 feet; upright habit.

CULTURE Hardy annual. Propagated by seed. Easy to grow in any well-drained loam soil in full sun.

DESCRIPTION White, umbrella-like flower clusters appear in summer, produce pungent seeds. Young leaves are oval with toothed edges. The name coriander usually refers to the seeds which are used sparingly to flavor many ethnic dishes, particularly Chinese, Mexican, and Italian. The names Chinese parsley and cilantro refer to the leaves which are generally chopped fine as a flavoring to soups and stews.

BOTANICAL NAME *Crocus sativus*

COMMON NAME Saffron

HEIGHT 4 to 6 inches; low, clump-forming habit.

CULTURE Hardy perennial bulb. Propagated by corms. Difficult to grow. Prefers a well-drained, fertile loam or sandy soil in full sun. Corms are usually planted in early summer, first producing spiky leaves and then fall-blooming flowers.

DESCRIPTION Blue or purple crocus flowers have conspicuous orange stigmas that hang over the petals. The long, pointed leaves are dark green, grasslike.

USES Cultivated for the orange stigmas that are cut, dried, and crushed into powder; used to flavor many ethnic foods, such as Indian (saffron rice), French (bouillabaisse), Spanish (paella), and Swedish (saffron bread). Since 10,000 flowers are needed to make one pound of saffron it is an extremely expensive herb. Saffron imparts an attractive yellow color to the dish being prepared, and was a source of beautiful yellow dye.

BOTANICAL NAME *Cymbopogon citratus*

COMMON NAME Lemon grass

HEIGHT 3 to 6 feet; clump-forming, upright habit.

CULTURE Tender perennial grass from the tropics. Propagated by division of the clumps in spring. Can be grown year-round outdoors only where winters are mild and frost-free. Usually grown in containers and taken indoors during winter. Before dividing, cut leaves back to just above the soil line. Prefers a well-drained, fertile loam soil in partial shade. Trim leaves to encourage tender new growth.

DESCRIPTION Rarely flowers. Leaves are long, slender, bright green, and slightly ridged.

USES Commercially cultivated in Florida for its strong, lemon-scented oil. Used in making many kinds of lemon-flavored candy. Leaves steeped in boiling water make a refreshing tea. Popular in Oriental cooking as a flavor enhancer and substitute for lemon.

BOTANICAL NAME *Dianthus gratianopolitanus*

COMMON NAME Cheddar Pink

HEIGHT 6 to 10 inches; low, mounded habit.

CULTURE Hardy perennial usually remaining evergreen through winter. Propagated by seed, cuttings, and division. Prefers a well-drained, sandy to loam soil in full sun.

DESCRIPTION Slender, blue-gray grasslike leaves form a dense mat creating an attractive ground cover. The showy, rosy pink flowers occur in spring.

USES The clove-scented flowers are used fresh and dried for potpourri. Popular ornamental for rock gardens and rock walls, also containers.

RELATED SPECIES *D. caryophyllus* ('Carnations') grown in Europe for perfumes.

BOTANICAL NAME *Digitalis purpurea*

COMMON NAME Foxglove

HEIGHT Up to 6 feet; slender, upright habit.

CULTURE Biennial. Usually dies after flowering, but re-seeds itself. Prefers moist, acidic soil in full sun or light shade.

DESCRIPTION Tall flower spikes are studded with tubular florets, usually purple in color, with conspicuous spotted throats. Soft, hairy, broad, pointed leaves are in basal rosettes. Native to Europe, but naturalized throughout the Pacific Northwest.

USES It is used medicinally as a heart stimulant known as digitalis, but only under a doctor's supervision. Popular for herb gardens because of its highly ornamental value. *Caution:* All parts of this plant should be considered poisonous if ingested.

BOTANICAL NAME *Dipsacus sylvestris*

COMMON NAME Teasel

HEIGHT 2 to 3 feet; upright, branching habit.

CULTURE Hardy biennial. Propagated from seed. Easy to grow in a wide range of soils, including impoverished soil. A common wayside weed throughout North America.

DESCRIPTION Cone-shaped flower heads studded with tiny lilac flowers appear in midsummer. The seed head dries, becomes hard, and is covered with curly spines. Leaves are pointed, thistlelike. Both stems and leaves are prickly.

USES The dried, prickly seed heads are used as a comb. They are also ornamental in dried flower arrangements.

BOTANICAL NAME *Elettaria cardamomum*

COMMON NAME Cardomon

HEIGHT 2 feet; spreading habit.

CULTURE Tender perennial. Propagated by division of rhizomes. Prefers fertile, moist loam soil in partial shade. Survives outdoors in winter only in mild-climate areas with little or no frost. Usually overwintered indoors in pots in Northern states.

DESCRIPTION Member of the ginger family. Broad, pointed, smooth green leaves hug the stem like a sheath. Small cream-colored flowers are borne on long horizontal stems, followed by seed cases that are triangular in shape and contain reddish brown seeds that emit a powerful, aromatic odor.

USES Mainly used as an ingredient in curry powder. Also pleasant to chew. In Russia, Norway, and Sweden cardomon is popular for flavoring cakes.

BOTANICAL NAME *Euphorbia lathyris*

COMMON NAME Mole plant

HEIGHT Up to 3 feet; stout, leafy, upright habit.

CULTURE Tender annual or biennial. Seed should be sown directly into the garden after danger of frost has passed, or from transplants started six weeks before outdoor sowing.

DESCRIPTION Stiff, erect, succulent stems are crowded with narrow, pointed leaves arranged in regimented alignment, one above the other. Inconspicuous flowers are nested in small bracts towards the top of the plant.

USES Its main value is as a repellent against infestations of moles, voles, gophers, and other animal soil pests. Generally planted in clumps around the perimeter of herb gardens and food plots. *Caution:* All parts of this plant should be considered poisonous.

BOTANICAL NAME *Ficus carica*

COMMON NAME Edible Fig

HEIGHT To 30 feet, usually, kept below 6 feet by pruning; shrub or treelike habit.

CULTURE Tender shrub or small tree mostly grown in tubs so it can be taken indoors during winter. Prefers fertile, well-drained loam soil in full sun. Heat and drought tolerant.

DESCRIPTION Large indented green leaves have prominent veins, are highly ornamental. Edible fruits are produced in the leaf joints, ripen in autumn, turning yellow, black, or brown depending on variety.

USES Grown extensively in herb gardens because of its presence in ancient monastery gardens and associations with the Bible. The ripe fruit is delicious eaten fresh, dried, and used in preserves.

RECOMMENDED VARIETIES 'Brown Turkey' (hardiest fig known—survives with protection to zone 5) and 'Mission' for mild winter areas.

BOTANICAL NAME *Foeniculum vulgare azoricum*

COMMON NAME Florence Fennel; Finocchio

HEIGHT 2 to 3 feet; feathery, upright habit.

CULTURE Hardy annual. Propagated from seed sown directly into the garden or started indoors six weeks before outdoor planting. Prefers a light, fertile soil in full sun. Cool weather is needed to form the bulbous lower stem section prized by gourmet cooks.

DESCRIPTION Resembles dill, except for its pale bulbous base and more compact growth habit. Slender, branching stems have fine, feathery leaves and yellow flower umbels. Its stems, leaves, and flowers are slightly more sweetly flavored than common fennel (*F. vulgare*).

USES Valuable flavor enhancer, especially in Italian cooking, imparting an aniselike flavor. With common fennel the seeds, leaves, stems, and flowers can be used to flavor soups, stews, and fish dishes. With Florence fennel, the crunchy bulbous base is used mostly to flavor salads, sliced like pieces of celery and used sparingly with salad greens.

BOTANICAL NAME *Galium odoratum* (also known as *Asperula odorata)*

COMMON NAME Sweet Woodruff

HEIGHT Up to 6 inches; low, ground-hugging habit.

CULTURE Hardy perennial. Propagated mostly by dividing clumps in spring or fall. Prefers a moist, humus-rich, loose soil in partial shade.

DESCRIPTION Small clusters of tiny, starry white flowers appear in spring among whorls of pointed leaves. The plant spreads rapidly and maintains a uniform height, making it a decorative ground cover.

USES An essential flavor enhancer for "May" wine. Once used for scattering on floors to sweeten musty rooms. Ornamentally, a valuable ground cover for shady areas. In autumn, when the leaves wilt and dry they pervade the air with a sweet hay-scented aroma.

BOTANICAL NAME *Heliotropium arborescens*

COMMON NAME Sweet Heliotrope; Common Heliotrope

HEIGHT 12 to 18 inches; erect habit.

CULTURE Tender annual. Seed should be started indoors and transplanted to the garden after danger of frost has passed. Prefers a fertile, moist, well-drained loam soil in full sun.

DESCRIPTION Clusters of fragrant violet-blue flowers are borne on brittle stems. Leaves are glossy, dark green, heavily veined, pointed. Flowers last all summer.

USES The vanilla scented flowers are used in the perfume industry. Plants are highly ornamental and popular for cutting.

BOTANICAL NAME *Hyssopus officinalis*

COMMON NAME Hyssop

HEIGHT 2 feet; shrubby, clump-forming habit.

CULTURE Hardy perennial. Propagated by seed sown directly into the garden or from cuttings. Prefers fertile, well-drained loam soil in full sun or light shade. If dry stems persist through winter, cut back to soil level in early spring.

DESCRIPTION Lavender-like flower spikes in blue, pink, or white bloom throughout summer. Aromatic leaves are narrow with a slightly musky aroma.

USES Oil from the leaves is used mostly in scented soaps and in potpourri. It is an important ingredient in Chartreuse liqueur. The strong aroma is considered a repellent against the cabbage butterfly. A tea from the leaves is said to ease discomfort from colds and indigestion. A popular component of herb gardens because of its ornamental flowers.

BOTANICAL NAME *Iris germanica* 'Florentina'

COMMON NAME Orris Root

HEIGHT 2 feet; clump-forming habit.

CULTURE Hardy perennial spreading by means of rhizomes. Propagated mostly by division of the rhizomes in autumn. Prefers a moist, well-drained soil in sun or partial shade.

DESCRIPTION Decorative flowers resemble those of *Iris germanica* ('Bearded iris'), usually white with a pale blue tint, possessing a spicy, pleasant fragrance. Slender, sword-shaped leaves emerge from the rhizomes in early spring, followed by flowers that may last two weeks.

USES When chopped into small pieces, or powdered and dried, the odorless rhizome becomes highly aromatic, with a sweet vanilla-like or violet-like fragrance. Mostly used as a fixative to preserve the fragrances of other herbs in potpourri and dried arrangements.

BOTANICAL NAME *Laurus nobilis*

COMMON NAME Sweet Bay; Laurel

HEIGHT Normally kept under 6 feet high by pruning, but in the wild it grows up to 40 feet high; forms an attractive bushy habit or tree.

CULTURE Tender evergreen shrub that must be overwintered under glass except in frost-free areas. Propagated by seed and by cuttings, though ready-grown plants are available from houseplant outlets. Best grown in a container with at least a one gallon capacity, using a fertile soil composed of equal parts of garden loam and potting soil.

DESCRIPTION Its tiny yellow flowers are borne in dainty clusters, though it rarely flowers in cold climates. The leaves are leathery in texture, shiny above, oval, and pointed, usually 3 to 4 inches long. Stems are upright, woody, and pliable. Often confused with California-laurel (*Umbellularia californica)* which has a stronger, harsher flavor and is not as desirable for culinary use.

USES Mostly used to flavor soups, stews, and sauces, one leaf to each gallon of liquid, simmered slowly to release its distinctive flavor. Traditionally used for "victory wreaths" to crown the heads of athletes and other people deserving high honors. The dried leaves have insect repellent properties and are popular for adding to potpourri.

BOTANICAL NAME *Lavandula angustifolia* (also known as *L. vera* and *L. officinalis*)

COMMON NAME English Lavender; True Lavender

HEIGHT 2 to 3 feet; bushy habit.

CULTURE Hardy perennial. Propagated from seed and cuttings. Easy to grow in any well-drained loam or sandy soil in full sun. Space plants 3 feet apart.

DESCRIPTION Lavender, pink, blue, or white flower clusters are borne on slender stems. Gray-green leaves are narrow, pointed. All plant parts are highly fragrant. Highly ornamental.

USES Mostly used air-dried to add distinctive fragrance to potpourri. Stems may also be steeped in boiling water to make a delicious tea. Lavender oil distilled from the flowering stems is used as a scent in soaps and perfumes.

RECOMMENDED VARIETIES 'Hidcote' (deep blue) and 'Jean Davis' (pink).

RELATED SPECIES *L. stoechas* ('French Lavender').

BOTANICAL NAME *Levisticum officinale*

COMMON NAME Lovage

HEIGHT Up to 6 feet; upright, clump-forming habit.

CULTURE Hardy perennial. Best grown by seeds sown directly into the garden in autumn, or started indoors six weeks before outdoor planting in spring. Prefers a deep, fertile, moist loam soil in full sun.

DESCRIPTION Small flower umbels, resembling dill flowers, are produced on celery-like plants in spring; become much taller and more invasive than garden celery. Produces brown seeds, thick roots.

USES All parts of the plant, including leaves, stems, roots, and seeds have culinary value, mostly as a flavor enhancer for salads, soups, stews, meat, and poultry. The roots can be steeped in boiling water to make a refreshing tea. Its reputation as a love potion is questionable. The flavor resembles celery.

BOTANICAL NAME *Marrubium vulgare*

COMMON NAME White Horehound; Candy Horehound

HEIGHT 2 feet; erect, clump-forming habit.

CULTURE Hardy perennial. Propagated mostly by seed. Tolerates poor, impoverished soils in full sun. Shear old plants in spring for a compact, bushy appearance. Divide overgrown clumps every three years.

DESCRIPTION Small white flowers bloom along the stems in summer. Gets its common name from the wrinkled, hoary appearance of the gray-green leaves, which have crinkled edges and curl down.

USES Mostly used to flavor candy. Leaves can be steeped in boiling water to make a refreshing tea said to relieve colds and sore throats. Popular in herb gardens because of its added ornamental value, especially as an edging or container planting.

RELATED SPECIES *Ballato nigra* ('Black Horehound') is much stronger in flavor and too harsh for most tastes, except as a strong tea.

BOTANICAL NAME *Melissa officinalis*

COMMON NAME Lemon-balm

HEIGHT 2 to 3 feet; mounded habit.

CULTURE Hardy perennial. Propagated by seed, cuttings, or root division. Prefers fertile, moist loam soil in full sun.

DESCRIPTION Related to mint, and very mintlike in general appearance. Leaves are bright green, heart-shaped, serrated, and heavily-veined. Small white flowers are borne along the stems in summer. Young plants form attractive compact mounds, but left unchecked it can become invasive.

USES The lemon-scented leaves make a delicious, refreshing tea steeped in boiling water. The leaves rubbed on hands act as a deodorizer, covering unpleasant smells such as fish and garlic. Dried leaves retain their aroma and are popular for adding to potpourri.

BOTANICAL NAME *Mentha piperita*

COMMON NAME Peppermint

HEIGHT Up to 3 feet; upright, clump-forming habit.

CULTURE Hardy perennial. Propagated mostly by cuttings and division of overgrown clumps. Prefers moist loam soil in full sun or light shade. Spreads quickly by underground rhizomes.

DESCRIPTION Erect, square stems with oval, pointed, serrated leaves. Pale lavender flower spikes appear in summer.

USES Commercially grown for its oil which is used to flavor candy, perfume, and potpourri. Rubbing the leaves between the palms covers objectionable odors, and inhaling the aroma clears the sinuses. Leaves steeped in boiling water make a refreshing tea.

BOTANICAL NAME *Mentha pulegium*

COMMON NAME Pennyroyal

HEIGHT 12 inches; spreading habit.

CULTURE Hardy perennial. Propagated by seed and by division of overgrown clumps. Tolerates a wide range of well-drained soils in full sun.

DESCRIPTION A member of the mint family. Leaves are small, oval, pointed, spaced evenly along slender stems with a dainty crown of pink flowers clustered at each leaf node.

USES Strong mint flavor reminiscent of peppermint. Its culinary use has diminished in recent years following reports that it can be toxic if used in excess. The leaves steeped in boiling water make a refreshing tea. Also adds a pleasant mint flavor to iced tea. Good to use as a natural insect repellent, dried and stuffed into sachets, or sprinkled over pet bedding.

BOTANICAL NAME *Mentha spicata*

COMMON NAME Spearmint

HEIGHT 3 feet; erect, bushy habit.

CULTURE Hardy perennial. Propagated by seed and root division. Any 3- to 4-inch section of root will produce a new plant. Prefers a moist loam soil in full sun or partial shade.

DESCRIPTION Pink flower clusters are borne at the top of erect stems in long, tapering spikes, usually in early summer. Narrow, pointed, bright green serrated leaves have conspicuous veins and are highly fragrant when bruised.

USES Spearmint is similar to peppermint in appearance and its list of uses, though it is milder. The oil is used as a flavoring by the cosmetics industry for everything from shampoo to toothpaste. Its culinary uses include flavoring iced tea, vinegar, fruit punch, and jelly. Mint cordials are common, as is mint tea.

RECOMMENDED VARIETY *Mentha spicata* 'Crispa' ('Curly-leaf Mint') has curly, quilted leaves that have ornamental value.

BOTANICAL NAME *Mentha suaveolens* (also known as *M. rotundifolia*)

COMMON NAME Apple Mint

HEIGHT 3 feet; upright, spreading habit.

CULTURE Hardy perennial. Propagated from seed, cuttings, and root division. Prefers moist loam soil in full sun. Tolerates dry conditions better than most other mints. Spreads by vigorous underground rhizomes, and generally needs thinning every year once a clump is established.

DESCRIPTION Typical mintlike appearance with heart-shaped, serrated leaves and square stems, though leaves are more rounded and have a woolly appearance with a distinct applelike aroma.

USES Mostly used in potpourri for its apple fragrance. Leaves can be candied and also used fresh or dried in cooking.

BOTANICAL NAME *Monarda citriodora*

COMMON NAME Lemon Mint; Lemon Bee-balm

HEIGHT 3 to 5 feet; bushy, clump-forming habit.

CULTURE Hardy perennial. Propagated mostly by division or cuttings taken in spring. Prefers moist, fertile soil in partial shade. Usually needs dividing every year after the third year.

DESCRIPTION Pale pink tubular flowers are arranged in a crown at the top of stiff, square stems. Leaves are oval and pointed and release a lemony aroma when bruised.

USES The fresh or dried leaves can be used as a flavoring in salads or steeped in boiling water to make a refreshing tea. Good also for potpourri. The flower display, which occurs in summer, is highly ornamental, attracting butterflies, hummingbirds, and bees.

BOTANICAL NAME *Monarda didyma*

COMMON NAME Scarlet Bee-balm; Bergamot; Oswego Tea

HEIGHT 3 to 5 feet; bushy; clump-forming habit.

CULTURE Hardy perennial. Propagated by seed, cuttings, and root division in spring or fall. Prefers fertile, moist, loam soil in full sun. Established clumps generally need dividing each year.

DESCRIPTION Red, tubular flowers are arranged in a crown on top of the plant in profusion; blooms July and August. Dark green, oval, pointed leaves have a citruslike aroma.

USES Mostly used for its leaves, which make a refreshing tea when steeped in boiling water. A prime ingredient in the making of Earl Grey tea. Highly ornamental for display. Attractive to butterflies, hummingbirds, and bees.

BOTANICAL NAME *Myrrhis odorata*

COMMON NAME Sweet Cicely; Myrrh

HEIGHT 5 feet; erect, branching habit.

CULTURE Hardy perennial. Propagated by seed or root division. Prefers a moist, humus-rich soil in partial shade. Plants self-seed easily.

DESCRIPTION The tall, sprawling plants somewhat resemble dill, but with white flower umbels. Related to parsley, the entire plant is aromatic, with a licorice-like flavor. In autumn the seed heads turn almost black, indicating ripeness. These are especially valued for culinary uses.

USES Pick young leaves for adding flavor to summer salads, and for steeping in boiling water to make a refreshing tea. The seeds can be used in baking to flavor pastries, and the fleshy root can be shredded to eat raw in salads or added to stir-fried vegetables.

BOTANICAL NAME *Nasturtium officinale*

COMMON NAME Watercress

HEIGHT 2 inches to 2 feet; spreading habit.

CULTURE Hardy biennial. Propagated by seed, by cuttings, and by division. Easy to grow in running water, though plants can be grown in moist soil in partial shade. Seeds need to be started in potting soil and then transplanted into water when large enough to stay anchored in running water. Stays low and floats on the water during cool weather; grows tall and runs to seed in hot weather.

DESCRIPTION Rounded dark green leaves form rosettes, succulent and pungent when young, developing a bitter taste with age. Each leaf node develops long, threadlike white roots which fasten to mud or sand along streams or springs. Flowers are white, dainty.

USES The young leaves are used fresh in salads and sandwiches, and as a garnish on meat, poultry, and fish dishes. The cooked greens can serve as a substitute for spinach, and watercress soup is a gourmet treat.

BOTANICAL NAME *Nepeta cataria*

COMMON NAME Catnip; Catmint

HEIGHT 3 feet; upright, branching habit.

CULTURE Hardy perennial. Propagated mostly by seed. Easy to grow even in poor soils, in full sun.

DESCRIPTION Masses of white flower spikes cover the gray-green plants in midsummer. Leaves are soft to touch, up to 2 inches long, pointed with toothed edges.

USES Cats enjoy sniffing and rubbing in catnip, which acts as a temporary euphoric on their senses. The leaves are sometimes dried and steeped in boiling water to make a soothing tea for humans.

BOTANICAL NAME *Nepeta mussinii*

COMMON NAME Catmint

HEIGHT 12 to 15 inches; low, spreading habit.

CULTURE Hardy perennial. Propagated by seed. Easy to grow in most well-drained loam soils in sun or partial shade.

DESCRIPTION Flowers consist of blue blossoms in tight clusters, appearing mostly in spring or early summer. Grayish leaves are rounded and soft to the touch.

USES Its gray foliage and ornamental blue flowers combine well, making catmint a good edging plant. The scent deters garden pests, but is attractive to bees. Commercially grown for its oil as an insect repellent. Unlike catnip, cats are indifferent to catmint.

RELATED SPECIES *Nepeta* x *faassenii* ('Ornamental catnip'): its deeper blue flowers produce an even better ornamental effect.

BOTANICAL NAME *Ocimum basilicum*

COMMON NAME Sweet Basil

HEIGHT 1 to 3 feet, depending on variety; bushy habit.

CULTURE Tender annual. Propagated by seed, best started indoors and transplanted into the garden after all danger of frost has passed. Easy to grow in any reasonably fertile, well-drained garden soil in full sun.

DESCRIPTION Common sweet basil has glossy, dark green, spear-shaped leaves with prominent leaf veins. Some varieties have curling, ruffled leaves, others tiny, rounded leaves forming a perfect mound. White flowers are borne in clusters on short spikes.

USES Fresh and dried leaves are used in a multitude of culinary dishes. It is the primary ingredient of pesto sauce and makes an excellent vinegar flavoring; it also goes well as a garnish with tomatoes.

RELATED SPECIES *Ocimum basilicum* 'Purpurascens,' (Dark Opal basil), a purple-leaf type popular as an ornamental in annual flower borders.

BOTANICAL NAME *Olea europaea*

COMMON NAME European Olive; Common Olive

HEIGHT 20 feet; bushy, multi-stemmed small tree.

CULTURE Tender evergreen tree that must be grown indoors in tubs over the winter in areas with freezing temperatures. Propagated mostly by cuttings. Tolerates poor soil in full sun.

DESCRIPTION Many varieties of European olive have been developed, including dwarf forms that can be trimmed into mounds and hedges. However, the common form is mostly grown in herb gardens to add height, particularly from its upright, twisting branches. The slender, willowlike leaves are an attractive gray-green. Tiny white flowers are followed by oval fruits that turn black when ripe.

USES Since the olive has strong associations with the Bible, it is popular in herb garden designs with an ecclesiastical emphasis. The oil from the pressed fruit produces olive oil enjoyed on salads. The fruit also makes tasty preserves for garnishing Greek and Italian dishes.

BOTANICAL NAME *Origanum majorana*

COMMON NAME Sweet Marjoram

HEIGHT 12 inches or more; tall, upright, bushy habit.

CULTURE Tender perennial usually grown as an annual. Propagated by seed, cuttings, and division. Prefers moist, reasonably fertile soil in full sun.

DESCRIPTION Small, oval green leaves are pungent and sweet, and are frost-hardy, but roots are sensitive to freezing. Clusters of small white flowers grow at the top of soft stems that turn woody with age.

USES Fresh or dried leaves are good to flavor omelettes and other egg dishes, also dishes involving mixed vegetables such as soups and stews.

BOTANICAL NAME *Origanum vulgare*

COMMON NAME Oregano; Wild Marjoram

HEIGHT 12 to 18 inches; bushy, erect habit.

CULTURE Hardy perennial. Propagated by seed, cuttings, and root divisions. Easy to grow in most well-drained loam soils in full sun.

DESCRIPTION Native American wayside plant. Similar in appearance to marjoram, except the small pink flower clusters are less conspicuous.

USES Fresh or dried leaves are used in a variety of dishes, especially pizza, cheese casseroles, and pastas, also tomato and spaghetti sauces.

BOTANICAL NAME *Panax quinquefolius*

COMMON NAME Ginseng

HEIGHT 12 to 18 inches; low, ground-cover effect.

CULTURE Hardy perennial. Propagated mostly by seed, though it is one of the slowest growing herbs in cultivation, requiring four years to flower and seed. Demands a moist, humus–rich soil in partial shade. A challenge to grow. Native to the Appalachian forest regions.

DESCRIPTION Five-pointed leaves surround a basal stem. Small greenish flowers appear on mature plants, followed by bright red berries. The plant develops a curious, fleshy tap-root often resembling a human form.

USES The powdered or shredded roots are dried to make a refreshing tea. The Chinese attribute mythical powers to ginseng as a medicinal cure-all for sexual potency; it is also a stimulant.

BOTANICAL NAME *Papaver rhoeas*

COMMON NAME Corn Poppy; Shirley Poppy

HEIGHT 3 feet; erect, clump-forming habit.

CULTURE Hardy annual. Best grown from seed sown directly into the garden where plants are to bloom since roots resent transplanting. Prefers moist sandy soil in full sun.

DESCRIPTION Shimmering, satinlike flowers in red, white, and pink are borne on wiry stems. Leaves are hairy, indented. By timing seed sowings to allow seventy days to bloom, plants will flower any time of year when nights are cool.

USES Flower pigments used as a coloring for medicine and wine. Plants are highly ornamental, especially planted in a mass.

BOTANICAL NAME *Pelargonium graveolens*

COMMON NAME Rose-scented Geranium; Deodorizer Plant

HEIGHT 12 inches or more; low, bushy habit.

CULTURE Tender perennial killed when ground freezes. Propagated mostly by stem cuttings. Grows in a wide range of garden soils in full sun or partial shade, as long as drainage is adequate. Mostly grown in containers so plants can be moved indoors over the winter. Can be kept compact and bushy by pruning.

DESCRIPTION Dark green, ruffled leaves are downy, soft to the touch, and release a spicy, rose-scented aroma. Flowers are borne in small clusters, in shades of pink.

USES The leaves are good, either fresh or dried, to flavor jellies, cakes, fruit punch, tea, and vinegars. Oil extracted from the leaves is distilled to make perfume. Popular for adding to potpourri. Leaves rubbed on hands mask unpleasant smells.

RELATED SPECIES There are hundreds of varieties of scented-leaf geraniums, including: *P. tomentosum* ('Wooly Pelargonium'), a peppermint-scented geranium; *P. odoratissimum* ('Apple Pelargonium'), an apple-scented geranium; *P. crispum* ('Finger Bowl Pelargonium'), a lemon-scented geranium; *P. fragrans* ('Fragrant Geranium'), a nutmeg-scented geranium; and *P. grossularoides*, a coconut-scented geranium.

BOTANICAL NAME *Perilla frutescens*

COMMON NAME Perilla; Beefsteak Plant

HEIGHT 3 to 4 feet; bushy habit.

CULTURE Tender annual. Seed can be sown directly in the garden or started indoors and transplanted after all danger of frost has passed. Tolerates poor soil, needs full sun or partial shade. Pinch growing tips to keep plants compact. Self-seeds easily. Tolerates high heat.

DESCRIPTION Shining, heavily-veined purple leaves resemble coleus. There is also a green-leafed variety that resembles nettle. Inconspicuous pale pink flowers may appear late in the season.

USES Young leaves are edible in salads, soup, and as a spinach substitute.

BOTANICAL NAME *Petroselinum crispum*

COMMON NAME Parsley

HEIGHT 12 inches; mound-like habit.

CULTURE Hardy biennial that sometimes remains evergreen even during freezing weather. Propagated by seed. Prefers a cool, humus-rich moist soil in sun or partial shade.

DESCRIPTION Dark green leaves are finely divided and curly, sometimes resembling a tight cushion of moss. Tiny clusters of greenish yellow flowers are produced on tall stems in the spring of the second year, setting seed and then dying.

USES An extremely popular garnish for all manner of culinary dishes, especially fish and potatoes. Sometimes used as an ornamental for edging flower beds.

RELATED SPECIES *Petroselinum crispum* 'Neopolitanum,' also known as 'Italian Parsley.'

BOTANICAL NAME *Pimpinella anisum*

COMMON NAME Anise

HEIGHT 2 feet; upright, slender habit.

CULTURE Hardy annual propagated from seed. Prefers a moist loam soil in full sun. Tolerates crowding.

DESCRIPTION Feathery green leaves resemble those of wild carrot. Umbels of white flower clusters resemble dill or Queen Anne's Lace, appear in summer. Entire plant has a licorice aroma.

USES The seeds can be collected and chewed to sweeten the breath and as a digestive aid. The seeds also yield a flavorful oil used in beverages, to add a licorice-like taste to candies and cookies, also to make a refreshing tea.

BOTANICAL NAME *Poncirus trifoliata*

COMMON NAME Hardy-orange

HEIGHT 10 to 15 feet; small, mound-shaped tree.

CULTURE Hardy deciduous shrub that becomes tree-like with age. Propagated by seed and softwood cuttings. Prefers a fertile, well-drained, acid soil in full sun.

DESCRIPTION Glossy, oval, dark green leaves resemble those of citrus. White orange-blossom flowers appear in spring, followed by round, orange fruits the size of golf balls, highly astringent and pleasantly fragrant, like lemon soap. The multi-branching stems are covered in sharp thorns.

USES The ripe fruits stay on the trees after the leaves have fallen in autumn, creating an ornamental effect either as a hedge or specimen. The fruits make beautiful indoor decorations, piled into bowls, where they release their aroma. They may also be studded with cloves to create fragrant pomanders.

BOTANICAL NAME *Poterium sanguisorba*

COMMON NAME Salad Burnet

HEIGHT 12 inches; low, mounded habit.

CULTURE Hardy perennial. Propagated by seed and division. Tolerates dry, sandy soil in full sun. Tolerates crowding. Self-seeds easily.

DESCRIPTION Long cascading stems splay out from the center of the plant, presenting the toothed, green leaves in matched pairs along each stem. Greenish flowers, small and inconspicuous, are produced in late summer.

USES The cucumber-flavored leaves are used in salads and vinegars.

BOTANICAL NAME *Punica granatum*

COMMON NAME Pomegranate

HEIGHT Up to 15 feet, usually kept below 6 feet by pruning; shrub or tree-like habit.

CULTURE Tender shrub or small tree. Propagated by cuttings. Tolerates a wide range of garden soils providing drainage is good, in full sun. Hardy to zone 7 outdoors, but mostly grown in tubs so it can be moved indoors for the winter.

DESCRIPTION Dark green, narrow, oblong leaves produced on woody stems. Lovely orange-red funnel-form flowers occur in summer, followed by shiny red fruit the size of tennis balls. A pulpy, succulent, fleshy area under the skin, surrounding the seeds, is edible.

USES Like figs, pear trees, and quince trees, the pomegranate was grown in ancient monastery gardens, and has become a traditional container plant for modern herb gardens. Considered a delicacy as a dessert fruit. Modern herbalists prize its long-lasting red fruits for decorating herbal wreaths.

BOTANICAL NAME *Rheum rhabarberum*

COMMON NAME Rhubarb

HEIGHT 2 to 3 feet or more; clump-forming habit.

CULTURE Hardy perennial. Propagated by seed and by root cuttings. Prefers moist, humus-rich, fertile soil in full sun. Thick clumps should be divided every four years.

DESCRIPTION Large, glossy, floppy leaves are borne on thick succulent stems colored green or red according to variety. Though the green part of the leaf is poisonous, the stem portion is edible if it is cooked. Flower spikes are large, bearing masses of creamy white blossoms.

USES The stems are generally cubed, boiled, and made into pie filling with sugar added to reduce the tartness.

BOTANICAL NAME *Rosa gallica* "officinalis"

COMMON NAME Apothecary Rose

HEIGHT 6 feet; shrubby habit.

CULTURE Hardy flowering shrub propagated by cuttings. Prefers fertile, moist loam soil in full sun. Flowers best when nights are cool.

DESCRIPTION Highly fragrant, deep pink, semi-double flowers measure 4 inches across, freely produced in early summer on vigorous plants with arching canes armed with prickly bristles and a few sharp thorns. Leaves are glossy dark green, oval, and pointed, with serrated edges. Attractive round red hips ripen in autumn.

USES Though petals of many fragrant roses are used in potpourri and for flavoring preserves, the 'Apothecary Rose' is the one rose favored above all others for the heavy substance of its petals, its long-lasting aroma, and the ability to retain its color. Easy to dry and candy.

BOTANICAL NAME *Rosmarinus officinalis*

COMMON NAME Rosemary

HEIGHT Up to 6 feet tall; shrubby habit.

CULTURE Tender perennial that remains evergreen in areas with mild winters. Develops woody stems with age and needs pruning to keep it compact. Prefers well-drained light soil in full sun. Popular container plant so it can be taken indoors over the winter.

DESCRIPTION Many ornamental varieties have been developed, including some with a weeping habit and others with a low, spreading habit. In the common variety, stems are stiff, upright, covered in needlelike leaves emitting a resinous, pinelike scent when rubbed. White or blue blossoms are small.

USES Popular herb garnish to flavor pork or ham. Steep leaves in boiling water to make a refreshing tea. Rosemary oil distilled from the leaves is used in perfume and shampoo. Many other uses are claimed medicinally. Good ingredient in potpourri.

BOTANICAL NAME *Rumex scutatus*

COMMON NAME French Sorrel

HEIGHT 2 feet; upright, clump-forming habit.

CULTURE Hardy perennial. Propagated by seed or root division. Tolerates poor soil, but flavor is enhanced by moist, fertile soil in full sun. To promote leafy growth, remove any flowers that form. Divide plants every three years.

DESCRIPTION Light green, spear-shaped leaves are wavy, growing upright from a basal clump. Flowers are greenish white, borne in loose spikes. The leaves are high in vitamins and impart a tangy, lemony flavor.

USES The leaves are chopped small to flavor soups and salads.

BOTANICAL NAME *Ruta graveolens*

COMMON NAME Rue

HEIGHT 2 to 3 feet; erect, bushy habit.

CULTURE Hardy perennial that sometimes remains evergreen throughout winter. Propagated by seed, by root cuttings, and by division. Prefers an acidic soil in full sun or partial shade. Tolerates poor soil.

DESCRIPTION Beautiful, indented blue-green leaves form attractive moundlike plants in spring, becoming more bushy and open as the season advances. Bright yellow flower clusters appear in midsummer.

USES Many of the medicinal claims made of rue are not now recognized as true. Today dried rue is used mostly as an insect repellent. The roots produce a rosy red dye. Popular in herb gardens for the ornamental value of its leaves, particularly the variety 'Blue Mound' and a variegated form with green and white leaves.

BOTANICAL NAME *Salvia elegans*

COMMON NAME Pineapple Sage

HEIGHT 2 to 3 feet; upright habit.

CULTURE Tender perennial. Propagated mostly from cuttings. Easy to grow in any well-drained garden soil in full sun. Needs pinching back to keep plants bushy and compact. Best grown in pots so it can be moved indoors during winter.

DESCRIPTION Beautiful tubular red flowers are borne on slender flower spikes in late summer. Stems turn woody with age. Green, spear-shaped leaves impart a pineapple fragrance.

USES Dried foliage is used in tea, potpourri, jam, and jelly. Flowers attractive to hummingbirds. Highly ornamental in bloom.

BOTANICAL NAME *Salvia officinalis*

COMMON NAME Garden Sage

HEIGHT 2 to 3 feet; bushy habit.

CULTURE Hardy perennial. Propagated by seed and by cuttings. Easy to grow in any well-drained garden soil.

DESCRIPTION Slender, oval leaves are gray, with a quilted texture, and highly aromatic when touched. Decorative flower spikes in white, pink, or light blue appear in spring.

USES Fresh sage leaves are more pungent than the dried leaves and should be used sparingly to flavor stuffing, sausage, vegetable dishes, and many other foods. Oil distilled from the leaves is used to make perfume.

RECOMMENDED VARIETIES 'Purpurescens' has purple leaves, and 'Tricolor' features white, pink, and purple leaves.

BOTANICAL NAME *Santolina chamaecyparissus*

COMMON NAME Gray Santolina; Lavender-cotton

HEIGHT 2 to 2½ feet; low, mound-shaped habit.

CULTURE Hardy perennial. Propagated by seed and cuttings. Prefers fertile, moist, well-drained acidic loam soil in full sun. During periods of high heat and humidity foliage may turn black. Roots need mulch protection during severe winters.

DESCRIPTION Attractive, silvery foliage is finely cut, making a mosslike cushion. In summer, masses of yellow, buttonlike blooms appear on slender stalks. Leaves are highly aromatic when touched.

USES Dried foliage repels insects, especially moths. Sensational edging plant for beds and borders.

RELATED SPECIES *Santolina virens,* 'Green santolina,' has dark green leaves and is hardier.

BOTANICAL NAME *Satureja hortensis*

COMMON NAME Summer Savory

HEIGHT 18 inches; bushy, spreading habit.

CULTURE Hardy perennial. Propagated by seed. Prefers fertile, well-drained loam soil in full sun. Self-seeds easily. Grows to be top-heavy as the season advances and may need staking for support.

DESCRIPTION Leaves are dark green, needlelike, crowded along wiry stems that become woody with age. Spikes of small pink flowers bloom in summer.

USES Fresh or dried leaves have a peppery flavor and are more potent than the related species, 'Winter Savory.' Used to flavor salad, vinegar, vegetable soup, and poultry.

RELATED SPECIES *S. douglasii,* 'Yerba Buena' , a native of California.

BOTANICAL NAME *Satureja montana*

COMMON NAME Winter Savory

HEIGHT 8 to 12 inches; low, spreading habit.

CULTURE Hardy perennial that stays evergreen except during severe winters. Prefers moist, sandy soil that is not too fertile, in full sun. The root crown is susceptible to rot in moist soils. Prune tops back in spring to keep the plant looking tidy.

DESCRIPTION Narrow, pointed green leaves are crowded along wiry stems. Plant is slow-growing and spreading. Short spikes of white flowers appear in late summer.

USES Milder flavor than Summer Savory, and is used the same way—to flavor salad, vegetable soup, vinegar, and poultry.

BOTANICAL NAME *Sesamum indicum*

COMMON NAME Sesame

HEIGHT 3 feet; upright, clump-forming habit.

CULTURE Tender annual. Propagated by seed. Prefers well-drained loam or sandy soil in full sun. Fast growing and difficult to grow in states with cool summers.

DESCRIPTION Resembles a giant nettle. Small, tubular, cream-colored flowers have broad, serrated, pointed leaves. Seeds, which are prized as a flavoring for Oriental dishes, soups, and cookies, are harvested when ripe, about five weeks after the flowers appear.

USES Soups and bakery products rely heavily on sesame seeds for their flavor. Seeds can be used whole, mixed into soups and stews, or crushed.

BOTANICAL NAME *Stachys byzantina, S. olympia*

COMMON NAME Lamb's-ears; Wooly Betony

HEIGHT 12 to 18 inches; low, ground-hugging habit.

CULTURE Hardy perennial. Propagated by division in spring. Prefers well-drained, fertile loam soil in full sun. Clear away winter-damaged foliage in spring.

DESCRIPTION Mats of soft, wooly, grayish white leaves resemble lamb's ears. In summer, spikes of pale pink flowers appear above the foliage.

USES Excellent for ground cover and edging. Grown mostly for its appealing silver color and velvety texture. Used extensively to help enhance herbal wreaths.

RECOMMENDED VARIETIES 'Silver Carpet,' a non-flowering form that remains low and spreading.

BOTANICAL NAME *Symphytum officinale*

COMMON NAME Comfrey

HEIGHT 3 to 4 feet; clump-forming habit.

CULTURE Hardy perennial. Propagated by seed and division. Prefers moist, fertile loam soil in full sun.

DESCRIPTION Big, dramatic leaves are dark green, heavily-veined, arching out from a basal crown. Pale pink tubular flowers are borne in summer on long stems. Needs pruning back after flowering.

USES A great number of medicinal remedies are attributed to comfrey, including relief from ulcers. In recent years, however, overdoses of chemical substances found in comfrey have caused cancer in rats. Its place in the herb garden today, therefore, has changed to emphasize its ornamental value, though traditional herbalists still do not hesitate to brew a cup of comfrey tea or add a chopped leaf to a spring salad.

BOTANICAL NAME *Tagetes erecta*

COMMON NAME American Marigold; African Marigold

HEIGHT 2 to 4 feet; erect habit.

CULTURE Tender annual grown mostly from seed started indoors and transplanted into the garden after danger of frost has passed. Prefers moist loam soil in full sun.

DESCRIPTION Serrated, dark green leaves have a spicy odor that repels foraging animals. Yellow or orange, fully double flowers up to 4 inches across are produced continuously all summer.

USES Petals are a substitute for saffron. The chemical xanthophyl, found in the petals, is fed to chickens to improve the cosmetic coloring of their breasts. The roots repel soil nematodes.

BOTANICAL NAME *Tanacetum vulgare*

COMMON NAME Tansy

HEIGHT 4 feet; dense, clump-forming habit.

CULTURE Hardy perennial. Propagated by seed and division. Easy to grow even in poor soil; prefers full sun. Spreads rapidly by underground rhizomes. Needs dividing annually after third year.

DESCRIPTION Dark green leaves are fernlike, pungent. Yellow buttonlike flowers appear in summer. Common wayside plant throughout North America.

USES Fresh and dried flower heads and foliage have insect repellent properties. Both leaves and flowers are beautiful in fresh or dried arrangements.

BOTANICAL NAME *Teucrium chamaedrys*

COMMON NAME Germander

HEIGHT 12 to 15 inches; low, bushy habit.

CULTURE Hardy perennial that stays evergreen in winter. Propagated by cuttings or division. Prefers fertile loam soil in full sun. In areas where winters are severe, plants benefit from mulching around roots.

DESCRIPTION Mature plants develop woody stems crowded with small, oval green leaves. Dainty pink flowers resembling thyme occur in midsummer. Plants tolerate crowding and can be planted to create a dwarf hedge.

USES A tea brewed from its leaves was thought to relieve gout. Today, its main value is as an edging plant for beds and borders; also to create knot designs and parterres.

BOTANICAL NAME *Thymus vulgaris*

COMMON NAME English Thyme; Common Thyme

HEIGHT 12 inches; mounded, shrubby habit.

CULTURE Hardy perennial that remains evergreen in winter. Cultivated by seed, cuttings, and division. Prefers a well-drained, garden loam soil in full sun.

DESCRIPTION Small, rounded green leaves create a bushy mound, covered in spring with clusters of showy pink flowers. Mature stems turn woody. Leaves are aromatic when touched.

USES The most popular culinary use for thyme is as a seasoning for vegetable, meat, and fish dishes. An essential ingredient in "Bouquet Garni," a cluster of five essential herbs tied together and steeped in soup or stew.

RELATED SPECIES *T. praecox* ('Creeping Thyme'), good for planting between flagstone; and *T. serpyllum* ('Lemon Thyme'), imparting a lemonlike aroma.

BOTANICAL NAME *Trigonella foenum-graecum*

COMMON NAME Fenugreek

HEIGHT 18 to 24 inches; erect habit.

CULTURE Tender annual propagated from seed. For curry-flavored sprouts, germinate seeds indoors on a moist paper towel in bright light. Outdoors, plants prefer fertile loam soil in full sun. Cold or moist soil induces root rot.

DESCRIPTION The brown, square-shaped seeds germinate quickly indoors and produce succulent sprouts with a mild curry flavor. Outdoors, mature plants produce cloverlike leaves and cream colored flowers in midsummer, followed by beaklike seed pods.

USES A primary ingredient of curry powder. Prized in Middle-Eastern cuisine to flavor curries, chutney, and candy. The sprouted seeds are good for sandwich fillings and salads. The ancient Egyptians attributed many medicinal benefits to fenugreek, including relief from colds and fever.

BOTANICAL NAME *Tropaeolum majus*

COMMON NAME Nasturtium

HEIGHT 2 feet for dwarf types, 6 feet for vining types; spreading habit.

CULTURE Tender annual grown from seed sown directly into the garden after danger of frost has passed. Flowers best when nights are cool. Tolerates a wide range of soil conditions in full sun. Rich soils produce more leaves, fewer flowers.

DESCRIPTION Bright green leaves resemble parasols. Flowers prolifically during cool weather. Color range includes yellow, orange, red, pink, and white. Dwarf cultivars trail beautifully to cover slopes. Climbing cultivars can be used on trellises.

USES Flowers and leaves are edible and impart a peppery flavor to salads. Seeds are edible, pickled as capers.

BOTANICAL NAME *Valeriana officinalis*

COMMON NAME Garden Valerian

HEIGHT 4 to 5 feet; erect habit.

CULTURE Hardy perennial. Propagated by seed and division. Prefers moist, well-drained loam soil in full sun or partial shade. Self-seeds easily. Sometimes needs staking.

DESCRIPTION Clusters of attractive white or pink flowers are borne on stiff stems in spring, imparting a vanilla-like fragrance. Finely divided leaves are blue-green and ornamental.

USES In ancient times the root was used medicinally to treat problems of the heart and central nervous system, such as hypertension and epilepsy. Today, the plant is used mostly for its ornamental effect.

BOTANICAL NAME *Viola odorata*

COMMON NAME Sweet Violet

HEIGHT 4 to 12 inches; low, clump-forming habit.

CULTURE Hardy perennial. Propagated from seed and division. Prefers moist, fertile loam soil in full sun or partial shade. Flowers best in spring and fall when nights are cool.

DESCRIPTION Showy flowers resemble miniature pansies, deep violet-blue in color. The dark green, heart-shaped leaves are also ornamental.

USES Oil distilled from the flowers is used in perfume. The candied flowers are sold commercially. Flowers are also added to jelly, salad, and fruit punch.

RECOMMENDED VARIETY 'Royal Robe,' growing large, long-stemmed purple flowers.

BOTANICAL NAME *Zingiber officinale*

COMMON NAME Ginger

HEIGHT 3 to 4 feet; erect, shrubby habit.

CULTURE Tender perennial native to the tropics. Propagated mostly by rhizomes and division. Mostly grown in tubs so it can be taken indoors during the winter. Prefers moist, fertile, humus-rich soil in sun or partial shade.

DESCRIPTION Slender, canelike stems grow erect, with broad, arching sword-shaped leaves. Yellow-green flowers with purple lips are arranged in a poker-straight spike. The fleshy underground rhizome is a source of ginger spice.

USES Invaluable flavor enhancer for spicy foods, particularly in Indian and Chinese cuisine. Also used to flavor drinks (ginger ale) and as candied preserves.

CHAPTER FOUR

GARDEN PLANS

HERB GARDENS CAN GENERALLY BE DEScribed as informal or formal in design. Informal gardens have free-form beds and borders with plants spilling over the edges onto meandering paths, usually composed of wood-chip mulch or stepping stones. Formal herb gardens are laid out in geometric lines—squares, circles, triangles, ovals, and rectangles.

Many herb gardens are designed to evoke a special theme. They can reflect a particular period—Medieval, Elizabethan, American Colonial, for example—they can form a special collection—all dye plants, all culinary, all fragrance. Herb gardens of all medicinal plants are called "Physick Gardens." Herbs also can be planted to create a color theme, especially 'silver' gardens using herbs with silvery leaves.

Herbs are very good to use in "sensory gardens" to provide enjoyment for the blind, since many have leaves with familiar fragrances and interesting textures.

The best herb gardens are designed for foliage effect more than flowering effect since the flowering display of most herbs is either inconspicious or short-lived. However, there are some notable exceptions—butterfly weed, lavender, and thyme—indeed, it's possible to create herb gardens as colorful as a bed of annuals or a perennial border.

No matter how small your garden space there's a garden design to suit it. The designs illustrated here can be adapted to confined places, and the plant suggestions can be changed to suit personal preferences.

BUTTERFLY HERB GARDEN

1. *Asclepias tuberosa* (Butterfly Milkweed)
2. *Digitalis purpurea* (Foxglove)
3. *Hyssopus officinalis* (Hyssop)
4. *Chrysanthemum coccineum* (Pyrethrum; Painted Daisy)
5. *Thymus vulgaris* (English Thyme; Common Thyme)
6. *Chrysanthemum parthenium* (Feverfew)
7. *Cichorium intybus* (Chicory)
8. *Heliotropum arborescens* (Sweet Heliotrope)
9. *Tagetes erecta* (American Marigold; African Marigold)
10. *Galium odoratum* (Sweet Woodruff)

11. *Allium schoenoprasum* (Chive)
12. *Calendula officinalis* (Pot-marigold)
13. *Achillea filipendulina* (Yarrow)
14. *Borago officinalis* (Borage)
15. *Artemisia absynthium* (Wormwood)
16. *Anethum graveolens* (Dill)
17. *Capsicum annuum* (Hot Pepper; Chili Pepper)
18. *Coriandrum sativum* (Coriander; Chinese Parsley; Cilantro)
19. *Dianthus gratianopolitanus* (Cheddar Pink)
20. *Foeniculum vulgare azoricum* (Florence Fennel; Finoccio)

21. *Iris germanica* 'Florentina' (Orris root)
22. *Viola odorata* (Sweet Violet)
23. *Stachys byzantina* (Lamb's-ears)
24. *Ruta graveolens* (Rue)
25. *Salvia officinalis* (Garden Sage)
26. *Crocus sativus* (Saffron)
27. *Rosmarinus offininalis* (Rosemary)
28. *Monarda didyma* (Scarlet Bee-balm; Bergamot; Oswego Tea)
29. *Mentha spicata* (Spearmint)
30. *Nepeta cataria* (Catmint)
31. *Rosa gallica* 'officinalis' (Apothecary Rose)

Left: a formal herb garden at the Dallas Botanical Garden in Texas is seen in mid-summer following nine weeks of severe drought. The herbs included here are white-flowering garlic, chives, and English thyme used as a ground-hugging carpet between the two lower beds.

ISLAND BED OF HERBS

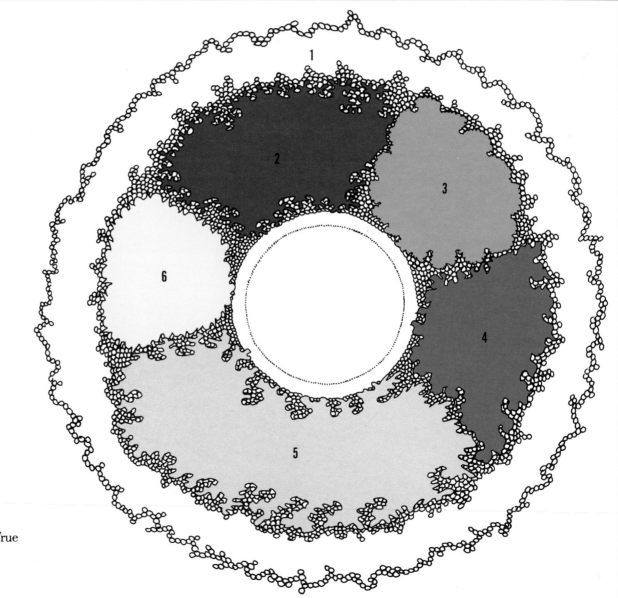

1. *Ocimum basilicum* (Sweet Basil)
2. *Hyssopus officinalis* (Hyssop)
3. *Artemisia dracunculus sativa* (Tarragon)
4. *Lavandula angustifolia* (English Lavender; True Lavender)
5. *Thymus vulgaris* (English Thyme)
6. *Ruta graveolens* (Rue)

Left: This birdbath serves as the focal point of this round island herb bed at Wyck House, a colonial herb, flower, and vegetable garden near Philadelphia, Pennsylvania. Yellow French marigolds yield petals that can be used as a substitute for saffron. The roses in the background are old-fashioned varieties, which yield highly fragrant petals when in bloom.

FREE-FORM BED OF FLOWERING HERBS

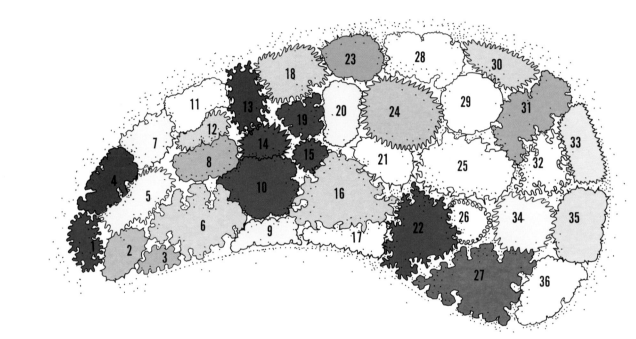

1. *Crocus sativus* (Saffron)
2. *Dianthus gratianopolitanus* (Cheddar Pink)
3. *Calendula officinalis* (Pot-marigold)
4. *Digitalis purpurea* (Foxglove)
5. *Chrysanthemum coccineum* (Pyrethrum; Painted Daisy)
6. *Lavandula angustifolia* (English Lavender; True Lavender)
7. *Anethum graveolens* (Dill)
8. *Asclepias tuberosa* (Butterfly Milkweed)
9. *Tropaeolum majus* (Nasturtium)
10. *Monarda didyma* (Scarlet Bee-balm; Bergamot; Oswego Tea)
11. *Allium tuberosum* (Chinese Chive; Garlic Chive)

12. *Allium schoenoprasum* (Chive)
13. *Agastache foeniculum* (Anise Hyssop)
14. *Camassia esculenta* (Quamash)
15. *Heliotropium arborescens* (Sweet Heliotrope; Common Heliotrope)
16. *Thymus vulgaris* (English Thyme; Common Thyme)
17. *Galium odoratum* (Sweet Woodruff)
18. *Rosa gallica* 'officinalis' (Apothecary Rose)
19. *Salvia elegans* (Pineapple Sage)
20. *Tagetes erecta* (American Marigold; African Marigold)
21. *Papaver rhoeas* (Shirley Poppy; Corn Poppy)
22. *Viola odorata* (Sweet Violet)
23. *Mentha spicata* (Spearmint)

24. *Santolina chamaecyparissus* (Lavender-cotton; Gray Santolina)
25. *Valeriana officinalis* (Garden Valerian)
26. *Satureja montana* (Winter Savory)
27. *Nepeta mussinii* (Catmint)
28. *Myrrhis odorata* (Sweet Cicely; Myrrh)
29. *Chrysanthemum parthenium* (Feverfew)
30. *Dipsacus sylvestris* (Teasel)
31. *Cichorium intybus* (Chicory)
32. *Capsicum annuum* (Chili Pepper; Hot Pepper)
33. *Anthemis tinctoria* (Golden Marguerite)
34. *Achillea filipendulina* (Yarrow)
35. *Alchemilla vulgaris* (Lady's-mantle)
36. *Catharanthus roseus* (Annual Vinca; Madagascar Periwinkle)

Left: This English teakwood bench is a good accent in this informal herb garden at the Chicago Botanical Garden, Illinois. A clump of large-leafed comfrey (left) and pink-flowered beebalm (right) flank the bench.

INFORMAL HERB BORDER

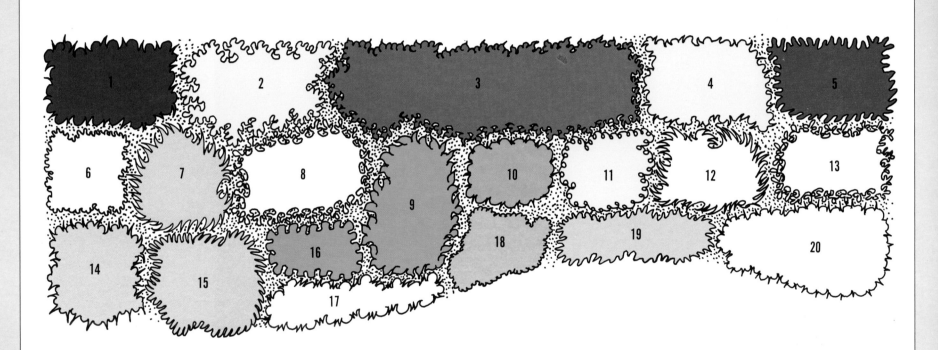

1. *Digitalis purpurea* (Foxglove)
2. *Anethum graveolens* (Dill)
3. *Lavandula angustifolia* (English Lavender; True Lavender)
4. *Achillea filipendulina* (Yarrow)
5. *Monarda didyma* (Scarlet Bee-balm; Bergamot; Oswego Tea)
6. *Salvia officinalis* (Garden Sage)
7. *Thymus vulgaris* (English Thyme)
8. *Valeriana officinalis* (Garden Valerian)
9. *Mentha spicata* (Spearmint)
10. *Cichorium intybus* (Chicory)

11. *Chamaemelum nobile* (True Chamomile; Roman Chamomile)
12. *Anthriscus cerefolium* (Chervil)
13. *Armoracia rusticana* (Horseradish)
14. *Allium schoenoprasum* (Chive)
15. *Borago officinalis* (Borage)
16. *Poterium sanguisorba* (Salad Burnet)
17. *Capsicum annuum* (Chili Pepper; Hot Pepper)
18. *Stachys byzantina* (Lamb's-ears)
19. *Dianthus gratianopolitanus* (Cheddar Pink)
20. *Satureja montana* (Winter Savory)

Left: This informal herb garden at Wave Hill Garden, near New York City, features a colorful assortment of foliage and many different textures.

TERRACED HERB GARDEN

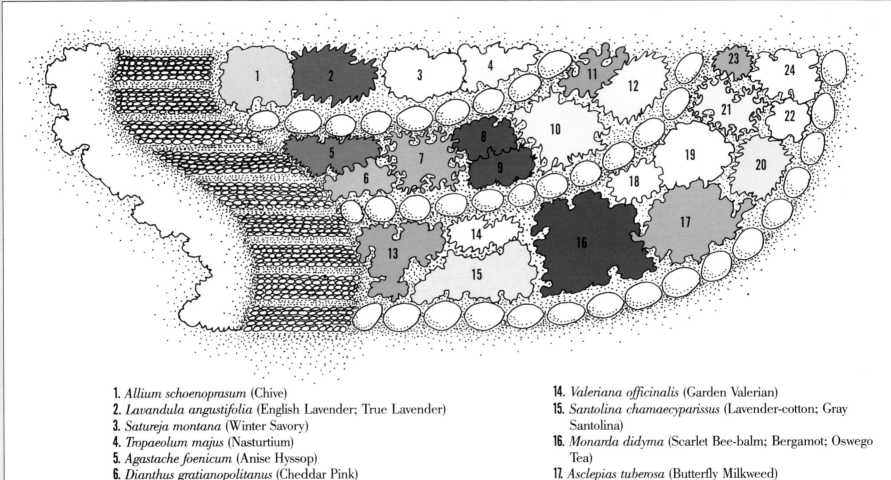

1. *Allium schoenoprasum* (Chive)
2. *Lavandula angustifolia* (English Lavender; True Lavender)
3. *Satureja montana* (Winter Savory)
4. *Tropaeolum majus* (Nasturtium)
5. *Agastache foenicum* (Anise Hyssop)
6. *Dianthus gratianopolitanus* (Cheddar Pink)
7. *Calendula officinalis* (Pot-marigold)
8. *Borago officinalis* (Borage)
9. *Crocus sativus* (Saffron Crocus)
10. *Achillea filipendulina* (Yarrow)
11. *Rumex scutatus* (French Sorrell)
12. *Ruta graveolens* (Rue)
13. *Rosmarinus officinalis* (Rosemary)

14. *Valeriana officinalis* (Garden Valerian)
15. *Santolina chamaecyparissus* (Lavender-cotton; Gray Santolina)
16. *Monarda didyma* (Scarlet Bee-balm; Bergamot; Oswego Tea)
17. *Asclepias tuberosa* (Butterfly Milkweed)
18. *Myrrhis odorata* (Sweet Cicely; Myrrh)
19. *Allium tuberosum* (Chinese Chive; Garlic Chive)
20. *Iris germanica* 'Florentina' (Orris Root)
21. *Foenicum vulgare azoricum* (Florence Fennel; Finocchio)
22. *Capsicum annuum* (Chili Pepper; Hot Pepper)
23. *Carthamus tinctorius* (Safflower)
24. *Armoracia rusticana* (Horseradish)

FORMAL HERB GARDEN

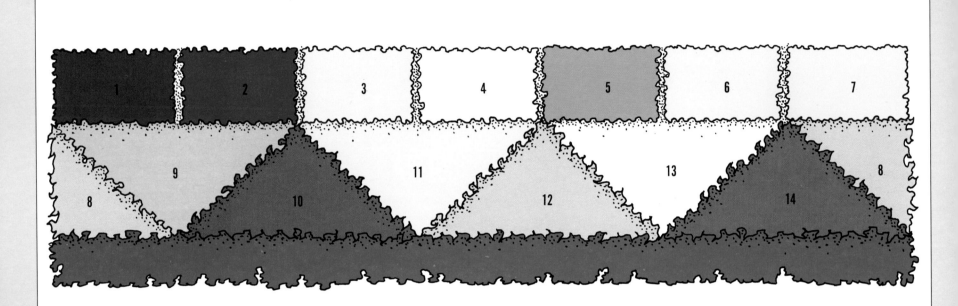

1. *Agastache foenicum* (Anise Hyssop)
2. *Monarda didyma* (Scarlet Bee-balm; Bergamot; Oswego Tea)
3. *Anethum graveolens* (Dill)
4. *Allium tuberosum* (Chinese Chive; Garlic Chive)
5. *Rosmarinus officinalis* (Rosemary)
6. *Tagetes erecta* (American Marigold; African Marigold)
7. *Chrysanthemum coccineum* (Pyrethrum; Painted Daisy)

8. *Allium schoenoprasum* (Chive)
9. *Stachys byzantina* (Lamb's-ears)
10. *Lavandula angustifolia* (English Lavender; True Lavender)
11. *Ruta graveolens* (Rue)
12. *Thymus vulgaris* (English Thyme; Common Thyme)
13. *Salvia officinalis* (Garden Sage)
14. *Hyssopus officinalis* (Hyssop)
15. *Petroselinum crispum* (Parsley)

Left: The historic herb garden at Trent House, Trenton, New Jersey, is enclosed by boxwood hedges.

FORMAL PARTERRE GARDEN OF HERBS

1. *Teucrium chamaedrys* (Germander)
2. *Salvia officinalis* (Garden Sage)
3. *Anthriscus cerefolium* (Chervil)
4. *Lavandula angustifolia* (English Lavender; True Lavender)
5. *Petroselinum crispum* (Parsley)
6. *Ruta graveolens* (Rue)
7. *Thymus vulgaris* (English Thyme; Common Thyme)
8. *Iris germanica* 'Florentina' (Orris Root)
9. *Chaemomilum nobile* (True Chamomile; Roman Chamomile)
10. *Anethum graveolens* (Dill)
11. *Stachys byzantina* (Lamb's-ears)
12. *Rosmarinus officinalis* (Rosemary)
13. *Mentha spicata* (Spearmint)
14. *Pelargonium graveolens* (Rose-scented Geranium; Deodorizer Plant)
15. *Rumex scutatus* (French Sorrel)
16. *Allium schoenoprasum* (Chive)
17. *Allium tuberosum* (Chinese Chive; Garlic Chive)

Left: A classical cartwheel design incorporates an intricate knot garden of herbs at the Matthaei Botanical Garden, Ann Arbor, Michigan. Green germander and silvery lavender form the dwarf hedges for the knot design. Yellow yarrow blooms in the foreground and rear.

KNOT GARDEN DESIGNS

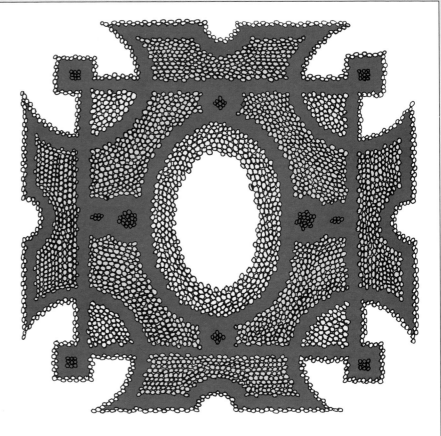

The two designs featured above appeared in a 1638 gardening book, entitled *The Country Housewife's Garden*, by William Lawson.

The following herbs, which are either low-growing or can be heavily pruned to form miniature hedges, are perfect for use in knot gardens.

Dianthus gratianopolitanus (Cheddar Pink)
Ocimum basilicum (Basil, especially Green Globe variety)
Lavandula angustifolia (English Lavender; True Lavender)

Ruta graveolens (Rue)
Salvia officinalis (Garden Sage)
Santolina chamaecyparis (Lavender-cotton; Gray Santolina)
Thymus vulgaris (English Thyme; Common Thyme)
Teucrium chamaedrys (Germander)

In addition to the above herbs, certain dwarf shrubs are also included in herbal knot gardens, including Dwarf Red Barberry (*Berberis buxifolia*) and Dwarf English Boxwood (*Buxus Sempervirens*).

Left: This walled herb garden at Agecroft Hall, Virginia, features Elizabethan-style knot gardens. Germander and lavender are used to form the knot patterns, while silvery lamb's ears edge the beds in the rear.

CULINARY HERB GARDEN

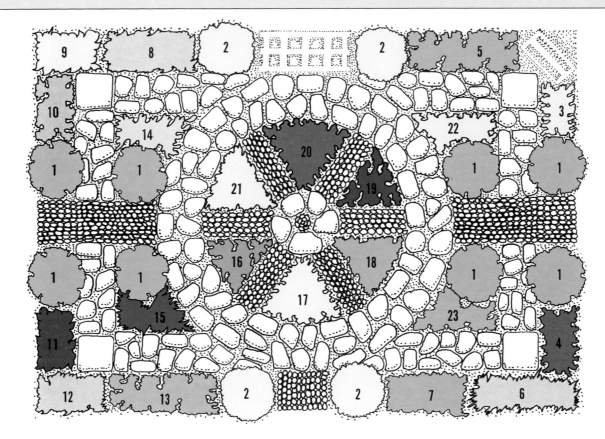

1. *Poncirus trifoliata* (Hardy-orange)
2. *Laurus nobilis* (in pots) (Sweet Bay; Laurel)
3. *Achillea filipendulina* (Yarrow)
4. *Lavandula angustifolia* (English Lavender; True Lavender)
5. *Capsicum annuum* (Chili Pepper; Hot Pepper)
6. *Allium schoenoprasum* (Chive)
7. *Allium tuberosum* (Garlic Chive; Chinese Chive)
8. *Thymus vulgaris* (English Thyme; Common Thyme)

9. *Chrysanthemuym coccineum* (Pyrethrum; Painted Daisy)
10. *Dianthus gratianopolitanus* (Cheddar Pink)
11. *Digitalis purpurea* (Foxglove)
12. *Dipsacus sylvestris* (Teasel)
13. *Asclepias tuberosa* (Butterfly Milkweed)
14. *Anthemis tinctoria* (Golden Marguerite)
15. *Salvia elegans* (Pineapple Sage)
16. *Rosmarinus officinalis* (Rosemary)

17. *Tagetes erecta* (American Marigold; African Marigold)
18. *Valeriana officinalis* (Garden Valerian)
19. *Monarda didyma* (Scarlet Bee-balm; Bergamot; Oswego Tea)
20. *Heliotropium arborescens* (Sweet Heliotrope; Common Heliotrope)
21. *Anethum graveolens* (Dill)
22. *Tropaeolum majus* (Nasturtium)
23. *Stachys byzantina* (Lamb's-ears)

Left: This knot garden of drought-tolerant herbs at Filioli Garden, Woodside, California, is seen in the heat of mid-summer. Green germander and silvery lavender form the dwarf hedges and dwarf myrtle forms the green mounds. Blue lavender is in bloom in the rear of the garden.

MINIATURE CULINARY HERB GARDEN

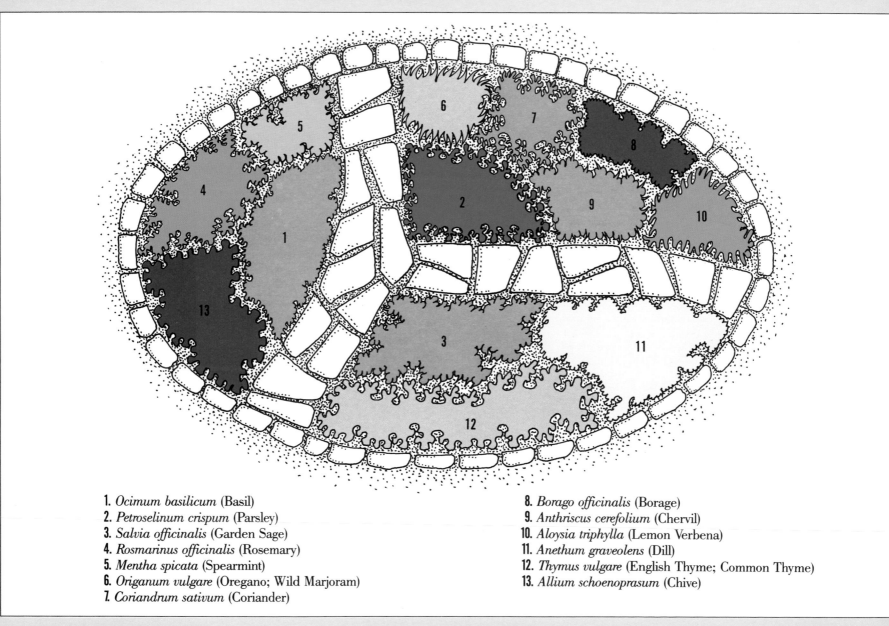

1. *Ocimum basilicum* (Basil)
2. *Petroselinum crispum* (Parsley)
3. *Salvia officinalis* (Garden Sage)
4. *Rosmarinus officinalis* (Rosemary)
5. *Mentha spicata* (Spearmint)
6. *Origanum vulgare* (Oregano; Wild Marjoram)
7. *Coriandrum sativum* (Coriander)

8. *Borago officinalis* (Borage)
9. *Anthriscus cerefolium* (Chervil)
10. *Aloysia triphylla* (Lemon Verbena)
11. *Anethum graveolens* (Dill)
12. *Thymus vulgare* (English Thyme; Common Thyme)
13. *Allium schoenoprasum* (Chive)

Left: A decorative lead hare, surrounded by clumps of chives, makes a whimsical focal point in this formal herb garden based on a cartwheel design. Scented-leaf geraniums decorate the urns.

FRAGRANCE & FLOWERING HERB GARDEN

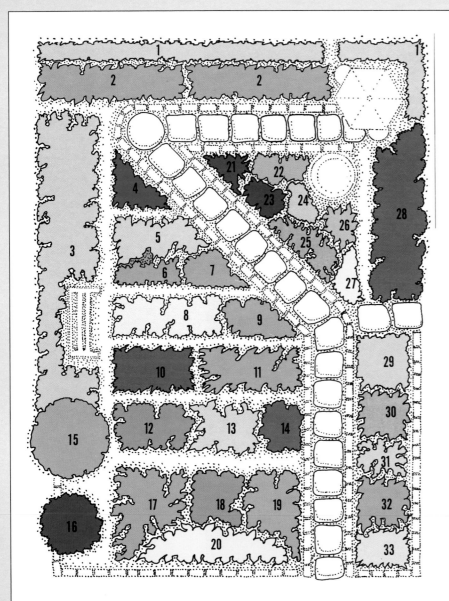

1. *Teucrium chamaedrys* (Germander)
2. *Capsicum annuum* (Chili Pepper; Hot Pepper)
3. *Rosa gallica* 'officinalis' (Apothecary Rose)
4. *Petroselinum crispum* (Parsley)
5. *Pelargonium graveolens* (Rose-Scented Geranium; Deodorizer Plant)
6. *Myrrhis odorata* (Sweet Cicely; Myrrh)
7. *Ocimum basilicum* (Basil)
8. *Monarda citriodora* (Lemon Bee-balm; Lemon Mint)
9. *Marrubium vulgare* (White Horehound; Candy Horehound)
10. *Mentha piperata* (Peppermint)
11. *Salvia officinalis* (Garden Sage)
12. *Artemisia dracunculus sativa* (Tarragon)
13. *Allium schoenoprasum* (Chive)
14. *Aloysia triphylla* (Lemon Verbena)
15. *Poncirus trifoliata* (Hardy-orange)
16. *Amorpha fruticosa angustifolia* (Indigo Bush; Bastard Indigo)
17. *Anthriscus cerefolium* (Chervil)
18. *Chenopodium bonus-henricus* (Good-King-Henry Goosefoot)
19. *Coriandrum sativum* (Coriander; Chinese Parsley; Cilantro)
20. *Anthemis nobilis* (Chamomile)
21. *Borago officinalis* (Borage)
22. *Asclepias tuberosa* (Butterfly Milkweed)
23. *Digitalis purpurea* (Foxglove)
24. *Dipsacus sylvestris* (Teasel)
25. *Santolina chamaecyparissus* (Lavender-cotton; Gray Santolina)
26. *Salvia elegans* (Pineapple Sage)
27. *Tagetes erecta* (American Marigold; African Marigold)
28. *Lavandula angustifolia* (English Lavender; True Lavender)
29. *Thymus vulgaris* (English Thyme; Common Thyme)
30. *Stachys byzantina* (Lamb's-ears)
31. *Papaver rhoeas* (Shirley Poppy; Corn Poppy)
32. *Origanum majorana* (Sweet Marjoram)
33. *Iris germanica* 'Florentina' (Orris Root)

Left: A colonial herb and vegetable garden on the estate of George Washington, in Mt. Vernon, Virginia.

Left: Raised beds edged with boulders allow assorted herbs to be grown on desert soil at the Boyce-Thompson Arboretum, near Superior, Arizona. Rosemary (left) spills onto the pathway, while clumps of healing plant *(Aloe vera)* and silvery artemisia decorate the beds in front of the stone wall.

PLANT SELECTION GUIDE

HERBS TO GROW FROM SEEDS

Achillea filipendulina (Yarrow)
Agrimonia eupatoria (Agrimony)
Allium species (Onion)
Aloysia triphylla (Lemon Verbena)
Anethum graveolens (Dill)
Angelica archangelica (Angelica)
Anthemis nobilis (Chamomile)
Anthriscus cerefolium (Chervil)
Artemisia absinthium (Wormwood)
Baptisia australis (False Indigo; Blue Wild Indigo)
Calendula officinalis (Pot-marigold)
Capsicum annuum (Hot Pepper, Chilli Pepper)
Carthamus tinctorius (Safflower)
Chenopodium bonus-henricus (Good-King-Henry Goosefoot)
Chrysanthemum species (Costmary; Pyrethrum; Feverfew)
Cichorium intybus (Chicory)
Coriandrum sativum (Coriander)
Digitalis species (Foxglove)
Dipsacus sylvestris (Teasel)
Elettaria cardamomum (Cardamon)
Foeniculum vulgare azoricum (Florence Fennel)
Galium odoratum (Sweet Woodruff)
Hyssopus officinalis (Hyssop)
Iris germanica 'Florentina' (Orris Root)
Lavandula angustifolia (English Lavender; True Lavender)

Marrubium vulgare (White Horehound; Candy Horehound)
Melissa officinalis (Lemon-balm)
Monarda citriodora (Lemon Mint; Lemon Bee-balm)
Monarda didyma (Scarlet Bee-balm; Bergamot; Oswego Tea)
Myrrhis odorata (Sweet Cicely; Myrrh)
Nasturtium officinale (Watercress)
Nepeta cataria (Catnip)
Nepeta mussinii (Catmint)
Ocimum basilicum (Sweet Basil)
Origanum majorana (Oregano; Wild Marjoram)
Panax quinquefolius (Ginseng)
Petroselinum crispum (Parsley)
Pimpinella anisum (Anise)
Poterium sanguisorba (Salad Burnet)
Rheum rhabarbarum (Rhubarb)
Rosmarinus officinalis (Rosemary)
Rumex scutatus (French Sorrel)
Salvia elegans (Pineapple Sage)
Salvia officinalis (Garden Sage)
Satureja hortensis (Summer Savory)
Satureja montana (Winter Savory)
Tagetes species (Marigold)
Tanacetum vulgare (Tansy)
Teucrium chamaedrys (Germander)
Thymus species (Thyme)
Trigonella foenum-graecum (Fenugreek)
Valeriana officinalis (Garden Valerian)
Viola odorata (Sweet Violet)

HERBS FOR SUN

Achillea filipendulina (Yarrow)
Agastache foeniculum (Anise Hyssop)
Agrimonia eupatoria (Agrimony)
Allium cepa proliferum (Egyptian Top Onion)
Allium fistulosum (Welsh Onion)
Allium schoenoprasum (Chive)
Allium tuberosum (Chinese Chive)
Aloe barbadensis (Healing Plant; Barbados Aloe)
Aloysia triphylla (Lemon Verbena)
Amaranthus hybridus hypochondriacus (Prince's-feather; Green Amaranth)
Armoracia rusticana (Horseradish)
Amorpha fruticosa angustifolia (Indigo Bush; Bastard Indigo)
Anethum graveolens (Dill)
Angelica archangelica (Angelica)
Anthemis nobilis (Chamomile)
Anthriscus cerefolium (Chervil)
Artemisia absinthium (Wormwood)
Artemisia dracunculus sativa (Tarragon)
Baptisia australis (False Indigo; Blue Wild Indigo)
Calendula officinalis (Pot-marigold)
Camassia quamash (Quamash)
Capsicum annuum (Hot Pepper, Chilli Pepper)
Carthamus tinctorius (Safflower)
Chrysanthemum balsamita (Costmary; Bible leaf)
Chrysanthemum coccineum (Pyrethrum; Painted Daisy)
Chrysanthemum parthenium (Feverfew)
Cichorium intybus (Chicory)
Coriandrum sativum (Chinese Parsley; Cilantro; Coriander)
Crocus sativus (Saffron)
Digitalis species (Foxglove)
Dipsacus sylvestris (Teasel)
Elettaria cardamomum (Cardamon)
Foeniculum vulgare azoricum (Florence Fennel)
Hyssopus officinalis (Hyssop)
Laurus nobilis (Laurel; Sweet Bay)
Lavandula angustifolia (English Lavender; True Lavender)
Levisticum officinalis (Lovage)
Marrubium vulgare (Candy Horehound; White Horehound)
Melissa officinalis (Lemon-balm)

Mentha peperita (Peppermint)
Mentha pulegium (Pennyroyal)
Mentha spicata (Spearmint)
Mentha suaveolens (Apple Mint)
Monarda citriodora (Lemon Mint)
Monarda didyma (Scarlet Bee-balm; Bergamot; Oswego Tea)
Nepeta cataria (Catnip)
Nepeta mussinii (Catmint)
Pelargonium graveolens (Rose-scented Geranium; Deodorizer Plant)
Petroselinum crispum (Parsley)
Pimpinella anisum (Anise)
Poncirus trifoliata (Hardy-orange)
Poterium sanguisorba (Salad Burnet)
Rheum rhabarbarum (Garden Rhubarb)
Rosarinus officinalis (Rosemary)
Rumex scutatus (French Sorrel)
Ruta graveolens (Rue)
Salvia elegans (Pineapple Sage)
Salvia officinalis (Garden Sage)
Santolina chamaecyparissus (Gray Santolina; Lavender-cotton)
Satureja hortensis (Summer Savory)
Satureja montana (Winter Savory)
Tagetes species (Marigold)
Tanacetum vulgare (Tansy)
Thymus praecox (Creeping Thyme)
Thymus serpyllum (Lemon Thyme)
Thymus vulgaris (English Thyme; Common Thyme)
Trigonella foenum-graecum (Fenugreek)
Valeriana officinalis (Garden Valerian)
Viola odorata (Sweet Violet)

Opposite page: This ecclesiastical herb garden at Carmel Mission, Carmel, California contains many of the herbs mentioned in the Bible. It features a fountain as a focal point.

Opposite page: An island bed of decorative summer-flowering herbs features silvery lamb's ears, yellow-flowering rue, white-flowering feverfew, and purple-flowered hyssop.

HERBS FOR SHADE

Agrimonia eupatoria (Agrimony)
Angelica archangelica (Angelica)
Anthriscus cerefolium (Chervil)
Armoracia rusticana (Horseradish)
Artemisia absinthium (Wormwood)
Chenopodium bonus-henricus (Good-King–Henry Goosefoot)
Cichorium intybus (Chicory)
Cymbopogon citratus (Lemon Grass)
Digitalis purpurea (Foxglove)
Galium odoratum (Sweet Woodruff)
Hyssopus officinalis (Hyssop)
Iris germanica 'Florentina' (Orris Root)
Laurus nobilis (Sweet Bay; Laurel)
Levisticum officinalis (Lovage)
Melissa officinalis (Lemon-balm)
Mentha piperita (Peppermint)
Mentha pulegium (Pennyroyal)
Mentha spicata (Spearmint)
Monarda didyma (Scarlet Bee-balm; Bergamot; Oswego Tea)
Myrrhis odorata (Sweet Cicely; Myrrh)
Nasturtium officinale (Watercress)
Nepeta cataria (Catnip)
Panax quinquefolius (Ginseng)
Rosmarinus officinalis (Rosemary)
Salvia elegans (Pineapple Sage)
Salvia officinalis (Garden Sage)
Tanacetum vulgare (Tansy)
Teucrium chamaedrys (Germander)
Valeriana officinalis (Garden Valerian)
Viola odorata (Sweet Violet)

HERBS WITH ATTRACTIVE FLOWERS

Achillea filipendulina (Yarrow)
Allium schoenoprasum (Chive)
Amaranthus hybridus hypochondriacus (Green Amaranth; Prince's-feather)
Baptisia australis (False Indigo; Blue Wild Indigo)
Calendula officinalis (Pot-marigold)
Cichorium intybus (Chicory)
Coriandrum sativum (Coriander)
Dianthus granitus (Spice Pink)
Digitalis species (Foxglove)
Dipsacus sylvestris (Teasel)
Hyssopus officinalis (Hyssop)
Iris germanica 'Florentina' (Orris Root)
Lavandula angustifolia (True Lavender; English Lavender)
Levisticum officinalis (Lovage)
Mentha suaveolens (Apple Mint)
Myrrhis odorata (Sweet Cicely; Myrrh)
Origanum vulgare (Oregano; Wild Marjoram)
Pelargonium graveolens (Rose-scented Geranium; Deodorizer Plant)
Poterium sanguisorba (Salad Burnet)
Rosmarinus officinalis (Rosemary)
Ruta graveolens (Rue)
Salvia officinalis (Garden Sage)
Satureja hortensis (Summer Savory)
Satureja montana (Winter Savory)
Tagetes species (Marigold)
Tanacetum vulgare (Tansy)
Thymus serpyllum (Lemon Thyme)
Valeriana officinalis (Garden Valerian)
Viola odorata (Sweet Violet)

COMMON
Stachys
Eurasia

HERBS FOR CONTAINERS

Allium schoenoprasum (Chive)
Aloe barbadensis (Barbados Aloe; Healing Plant)
Aloysia triphylla (Lemon Verbena)
Amaranthus hybridus hypochondriacus (Prince's-feather;
    Green Amaranth)
Anethum graveolens (Dill)
Anthemis nobilis (Chamomile)
Anthriscus cerefolium (Chervil)
Artemisia dracunculus sativa (Tarragon)
Calendula officinalis (Pot-marigold)
Cichorium intybus (Chicory)
Coriandrum sativum (Coriander)
Euphorbia lathyris (Mole plant)
Foeniculum vulgare azoricum (Florence Fennel)
Galium odoratum (Sweet Woodruff)
Hyssopus officinalis (Hyssop)
Laurus nobilis (Laurel; Sweet Bay)
Lavandula angustifolia (English Lavender;
    True Lavender)
Marrubium vulgare (White Horehound;
    Candy Horehound)
Melissa officinalis (Lemon-balm)
Mentha species (Mint)
Nepeta cataria (Catnip)
Nepeta mussinii (Catmint)
Ocimum basilicum (Sweet Basil)
Origanum majorana (Sweet Marjoram)
Origanum vulgare (Oregano; Wild Marjoram)
Pelargonium graveolens (Rose-scented Geranium;
    Deodorizer Plant)
Petroselinum crispum (Parsley)
Poterium sanguisorba (Salad Burnet)
Rosmarinus officinalis (Rosemary)
Rumex scutatus (French Sorrel)
Ruta graveolens (Rue)
Salvia elegans (Pineapple Sage)
Salvia officinalis (Garden Sage)
Satureja hortensis (Summer Savory)
Satureja montana (Winter Savory)
Tagetes species (Marigold)
Teucrium chamaedrys (Germander)
Thymus species (Thyme)

HERBS FOR CULINARY USE

Agastache foeniculum (Anise Hyssop)
Allium species (Onion)
Anethum graveolens (Dill)
Angelica archangelica (Angelica)
Anthemis nobilis (Chamomile)
Anthriscus cerefolium (Chervil)
Armoracia rusticana (Horseradish)
Artemisia dracunculus sativa (Tarragon)
Borago officinalis (Borage)
Capsicum annuum (Hot Pepper; Chilli Pepper)
Carthamus tinctorius (Safflower)
Chenopodium bonus-henricus (Good-King-Henry
    Goosefoot)
Chrysanthemum balsamita (Costmary)
Cichorium intybus (Chicory)
Coriandrum sativum (Coriander)
Crocus sativus (Saffron)
Elettaria cardamomum (Cardamon)
Foeniculum vulgare azoricum (Fennel)
Laurus nobilis (Sweet Bay; Laurel)
Levisticum officinale (Lovage)
Melissa officinalis (Lemon-balm)
Mentha species (Mint) except *M. pulegium* (Pennyroyal)
Monarda didyma (Scarlet Bee-balm; Bergamot; Oswego
    Tea)
Nasturtium officinale (Watercress)
Ocimum basilicum (Sweet Basil)
Olea europaea (Common Olive; European Olive)
Origanum majorana (Sweet Marjoram)
Origanum vulgare (Oregano; Wild Marjoram)
Pelargonium graveolens (Rose-scented Geranium;
    Deodorizer Plant)
Petroselinum crispum (Parsley)
Pimpinella anisum (Anise)
Poterium sanguisorba (Salad Burnet)
Rheum rhabarbarum (Rhubarb)
Rosmarinus officinalis (Rosemary)
Rumex scutatus (French Sorrel)
Salvia officinalis (Garden Sage)
Satureja hortensis (Summer Savory)
Satureja montana (Winter Savory)
Thymus species (Thyme)
Trigonella foenum-graecum (Fenugreek)
Viola odorata (Sweet Violet)

Opposite page: A pair of scented-leaf geraniums in pots crown the stone walls; other potted herbs provide culinary flavors for the kitchen, located right off of the patio. The close proximity of the garden to the kitchen makes it easier for the cook to clip the herbs needed for the dish being prepared.

Opposite page: A walled garden, grown in raised beds filled with humus-rich soil, provides shelter and ideal growing conditions for herbs.

HERBS FOR FLAVORING

Angelica *(Angelica archangelica):* breads, fruit, jellies, teas

Basil *(Ocimum basilicum):* breads, butters, cheeses, eggs, meats, salads, sauces, vegetables, vinegars

Burnet *(Poterium sanguisorba):* cheeses, eggs, salads, vegetables, vinegars

Caraway *(Carum carvi):* breads, cheese, meats, vegetables

Chervil *(Anthriscus cerefolium):* breads, butters, cheeses, eggs, fish, meats, vegetables

Chives *(Allium schoenoprasum):* breads, butters, cheeses, eggs, fish, meats, salads, sauces, teas

Sweet Cicely *(Myrrhis odorata):* breads, butters, cheeses, eggs, fish, fruits, jellies, meats, salads, sauces, tea, vegetables

Dill *(Anethum graveolens):* breads, butters, cheeses, eggs, fish, meats, salads, sauces, vegetables, vinegars

Fennel *(Foeniculum vulgare azoricum):* meats, sauces, vegetables

Lovage *(Levisticum officinale):* salads, sauces, vegetables, vinegars

Marjoram *(Origanum* species): breads, butters, cheeses, meats, salads, sauces, vegetables

Mint *(Mentha* species): breads, butters, fruits, jellies, meats, salads, sauces, vegetables

Oregano *(Origanum vulgare):* breads, butters, cheeses, eggs, meats, salads, sauces, vegetables

Parsley *(Petroselinum crispum:* breads, butters, cheeses, eggs, fish, salads, sauces, vegetables

Rosemary *(Rosmarinus officinalis):* breads, butters, cheeses, eggs, fish, fruits, meats, sauces, teas, vegetables

Sage *(Salvia officinalis):* breads, butters, cheeses, meats, sauces, teas

Savory *(Saturea hortensis* or *S. montana):* breads, butters, cheeses, eggs, meats, salads, sauces, vegetables

Tarragon *(Artemisia dracunculus sativa):* breads, butters, cheeses, eggs, fish, meats, salads, sauces, vegetables, vinegars

Thyme *(Thymus* species): breads, butters, cheeses, eggs, fish, meats, salads, sauces, vegetables, vinegars

HERBAL BUTTERS

Allium schoenoprasum (Chive)
Anethum graveolens (Dill)
Anthriscus cerefolium (Chervil)
Armoracia rusticana (Horseradish)
Artemisia dracunculus sativa (Tarragon)
Mentha species (Mint)
Myrrhis odorata (Sweet Cicely; Myrrh)
Ocimum basilicum (Sweet Basil)
Origanum majorana (Sweet Marjoram)
Origanum vulgare (Oregano; Wild Marjoram)
Petroselinum crispum (Parsley)
Rosmarinus officinalis (Rosemary)
Salvia officinalis (Garden Sage)
Satureja hortensis (Summer Savory)
Satureja montana (Winter Savory)
Thymus species (Thyme)

HERBS FOR TEA

Achillea filipendulina (Yarrow)
Agrimonia eupatoria (Agrimony)
Anthemis nobilis (Chamomile)
Borago officinalis (Borage)
Cymbopogon citratus (Lemon Grass)
Foeniculum vulgare azoricum (Florence Fennel)
Hyssopus officinalis (Hyssop)
Laurus nobilis (Sweet Bay; Laurel)
Marrubium vulgare (White Horehound; Candy Horehound)
Melissa officinalis (Lemon-balm)
Mentha species (Mint)
Monarda citriodora (Lemon Mint)
Monarda didyma (Scarlet Bee-balm; Bergamot; Oswego Tea)
Nepeta cataria (Catnip)
Ocimum basilicum (Sweet Basil)
Origanum vulgare (Wild Marjoram)
Salvia officinalis (Pineapple Sage)
Satureja hortensis (Summer Savory)
Satureja montana (Winter Savory)
Symphytum officinale (Comfrey)
Thymus species (Thyme)

HERBS FOR VINEGARS

Allium schoenoprasum (Chives)
Anethum graveolens (Dill)
Artemisia dracunculus sativa (Tarragon)
Levisticum officinale (Lovage)
Ocimum basilicum (Sweet Basil)
Origanum majorana (Sweet Marjoram)
Origanum vulgare (Wild Marjoram)
Petroselinum crispum (Parsley)
Poterium sanguisorba (Salad Burnet)
Rosmarinus officinalis (Rosemary)
Salvia officinalis (Garden Sage)
Thymus species (Thyme)

HERBS FOR FRAGRANCE AND POTPOURRIS

Agastache foeniculum (Anise Hyssop)
Agrimonia eupatoria (Agrimony)
Angelica archangelica (Angelica)
Anthemis nobilis (Chamomile)
Artemisia absinthium (Wormwood)
Chrysanthemum balsamita (Costmary)
Coriandrum sativum (Coriander)
Foeniculum vulgare azoricum (Florence Fennel)
Iris germanica 'Florentina' (Orris Root)
Laurus nobilis (Sweet Bay; Laurel)
Lavandula angustifolia (English Lavender)
Melissa officinalis (Lemon-balm)
Mentha species (Mint)
Monarda citriodora (Lemon Mint)
Monarda didyma (Scarlet Bee-balm; Bergamot; Oswego Tea)
Myrrhis odorata (Sweet Cicely; Myrrh)
Nepeta cataria (Catnip)
Ocimum basilicum (Sweet Basil)
Origanum majorana (Sweet Marjoram)
Pelargonium graveolens (Rose-scented Geranium; Deodorizer Plant)
Pimpinella anisum (Anise)
Rosmarinus officinalis (Rosemary)
Salvia elegans (Pineapple Sage)
Salvia officinalis (Garden Sage)

Santolina chamaecyparissus (Gray Santolina; Lavender-cotton)
Satureja hortensis (Summer Savory)
Satureja montana (Winter Savory)
Thymus species (Thyme)
Viola odorata (Sweet Violet)

HERBS FOR DRYING

Amaranthus hybridus hypochondriacus (Prince's-feather; Green Amaranth)
Anthemis nobilis (Chamomile)
Anthriscus cerefolium (Chervil)
Artemisia dracunculus sativa (Tarragon)
Carthamus tinctorius (Safflower)
Chrysanthemum balsamita (Costmary)
Chrysanthemum parthenium (Feverfew)
Coriandrum sativum (Coriander)
Dipsacus sylvestris (Teasel)
Iris germanica 'Florentina' (Orris Root)
Lavandula angustifolia (English Lavender; True Lavender)
Laurus nobilis (Sweet Bay; Laurel)
Levisticum officinale (Lovage)
Melissa officinalis (Lemon-balm)
Mentha species (Mint)
Monarda citriodora (Lemon Mint)
Monarda didyma (Scarlet Bee-balm; Bergamot; Oswego Tea)
Ocimum basilicum (Sweet Basil)
Origanum majorana (Sweet Marjoram)
Origanum vulgare (Oregano; Wild Marjoram)
Nepeta cataria (Catnip)
Pimpinella anisum (Anise)
Rosmarinus officinalis (Rosemary)
Ruta graveolens (Rue)
Salvia elegans (Pineapple Sage)
Salvia officinalis (Sage)
Satureja hortensis (Summer Savory)
Satureja montana (Winter Savory)
Symphytum officinale (Comfrey)
Tanacetum vulgare (Tansy)
Thymus species (Thyme)
Trigonella foenum-graecum (Fenugreek)
Valeriana officinalis (Garden Valerian)

Opposite page: Beds of herbs planted to overflowing at Wave Hill Garden, near New York City.

HERBS FOR DYES

HERB	COLOR
Achillea fillipendulina (Yarrow)	green
Agrimonia eupatoria (Agrimony)	yellow
Alchemilla mollis (Lady's Mantle)	green
Allium cepa proliferum (Egyptian Top Onion)	yellow-orange
Anethum graveolens (Dill)	green
Anthemis nobilis (Chamomile)	buff to gold
Baptisia australis (Blue Wild Indigo)	blue
Carthamus tinctorius (Safflower)	pink, orange, yellow
Chamaemelium nobile (Chamomile)	yellow
Crocus sarvus (Saffron)	yellow
Foeniculum vulgare azoricum (Florence Fennel)	bright yellow, gold
Galium odoratum (Sweet Woodruff)	yellow
Iris germanica 'Florentina' (Orris Root)	blue
Nepeta cataria (Catnip)	light yellow, gray-gold
Origanum vulgare (Wild Marjoram)	red
Petroselinum crispum (Parsley)	golden green yellow
Ruta graveolens (Common Rue)	yellow, green
Symphytum officinale (Comfrey)	green
Tagetes species (Marigolds)	lemon-yellow, bright orange
Tanacetum vulgare (Common Tansy)	green, yellow, brown

HERBS FOR MEDICINAL USES

Aloe barbadensis (Healing Plant; Barbados Aloe)
Anthemis nobilis (Chamomile)
Borago officinalis (Borage)
Cichorium intybus (Chicory)
Digitalis species (Foxglove)
Hyssopus officinalis (Hyssop)
Marrubium vulgare (Horehound; Candy Horehound)
Melissa officinalis (Lemon-balm)
Mentha species (Mint)
Ocimum basilicum (Sweet Basil)
Panax quinquefolius (Ginseng)
Pimpinella anisum (Anise)
Poterium sanguisorba (Salad Burnet)
Rheum rhabarbarum (Rhubarb)
Rosmarinus officinalis (Rosemary)
Ruta graveolens (Rue)
Satureja hortensis (Summer Savory)
Thymus species (Thyme)
Valeriana officinalis (Garden Valerian)

HARDINESS ZONE CHART

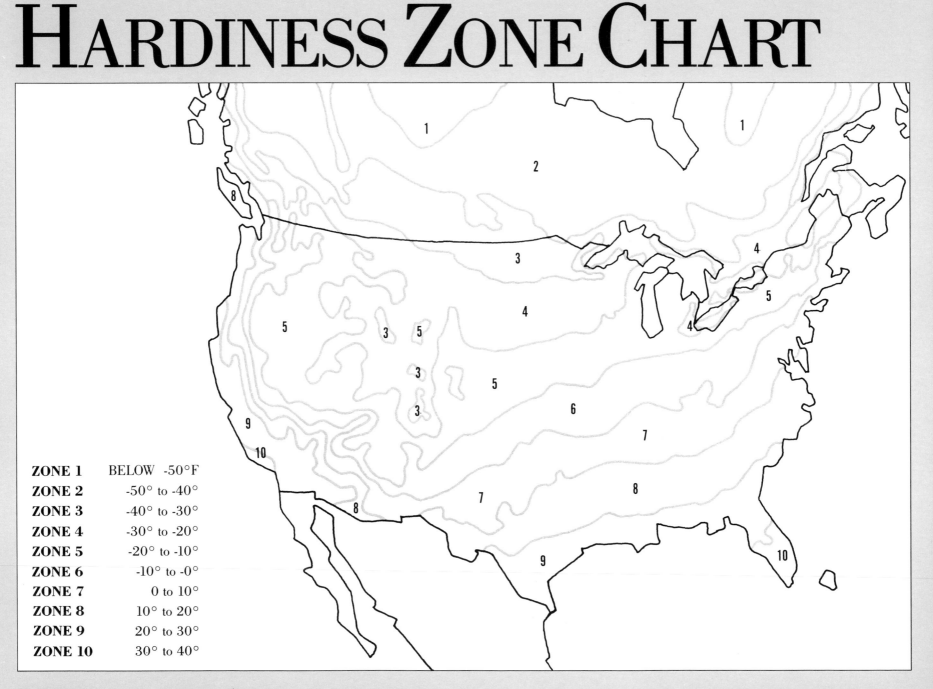

ZONE 1	BELOW -50°F
ZONE 2	-50° to -40°
ZONE 3	-40° to -30°
ZONE 4	-30° to -20°
ZONE 5	-20° to -10°
ZONE 6	-10° to -0°
ZONE 7	0 to 10°
ZONE 8	10° to 20°
ZONE 9	20° to 30°
ZONE 10	30° to 40°

Left: At Meadowbrook Farm, near Philadelphia, Pennsylvania, a formal herb garden containing sorrel, garlic chives, and various varieties of lettuce, is accented with a metal sundial and wrought-iron benches.

SOURCES

THE FOLLOWING MAIL order specialists provide either herb seeds or plants. Send for their catalogs.

ABUNDANT LIFE SEED FOUNDATION
Box 771
1029 Lawrence
Port Townsend, WA 98368
Offers a wide selection of herb seeds. Catalog $1.00.

W. ATLEE BURPEE COMPANY
300 Park Avenue
Warminster, PA 18974
Offers both herb seeds and plants. Catalog free.

CAPRILANDS HERB FARM
Silver Street
North Coventry, CT 06238
Offers herb plants. Catalog free with stamped, self-addressed envelope. Display gardens open to the public.

CARROLL GARDENS
Box 310
Westminster, MD 21157
Offers perennial herb plants. Catalog $2.00.

COMSTOCK, FERRE & COMPANY
Box 125
Wethersfield, CT 06109
Offers herb seeds. Catalog free.

THE COOK'S GARDEN
Box 65
Moffits Bridge
Londonderry, VT 05148
Offers on extensive selection of herbs. Catalog $1.00.

FOX HILL FARM
440 West Michigan Avenue
Parma, MI 49269
Offers 350 varieties of herbs and scented geraniums. Catalog $1.00.

LE JARDIN DU GOURMET
Box 44
West Danville, VT 05873-0044
Features packets of herb seeds at low cost. Catalog 50¢.

NICHOLS GARDEN NURSERY
1190 North Pacific Highway
Albany, OR 97321
Offers herbs to grow from seed. Catalog free.

GEO. W. PARK SEED COMPANY
Box 31
398 Cokesbury Road
Greenwood, SC 29647
Features herbs to grow from seed. Catalog free.

PINETREE GARDEN SEEDS
Route 100 North
New Gloucester, ME 04260
Features many herbs to grow from seed. Catalog free.

REDWOOD CITY SEED COMPANY
Box 361
Redwood City, CA 94064
Offers herbs to grow from seed. Catalog 50¢.

ROSES OF YESTERDAY & TODAY
802 Brown's Valley Road
Watsonville, CA 95076
Offers fragrant and old fashioned roses for potpourri. Catalog $1.00.

THOMPSON & MORGAN
Box 1308
Juckson, NJ 08527
Offers herb seeds. Catalog free.

WELL-SWEEP HERB FARM
317 Mt. Bethel Road
Port Murray, NJ 07865
Offers herb plants. Catalog $1.00. Display gardens open to the public.

Opposite page: The herb garden at The Cloisters, in New York City, features herbs, such as quince trees, that were grown in Medieval monastery gardens.
Left: A corner of the National Herb Garden at the United States National Arboretum in Washington DC

Index Of Botanical And Common Names

Pennyroyal. *See Mentha pulegium*
Pepper. *See Capsicum annum*
Peppermint. *See Mentha piperita*
Perilla. *See Perilla frutescens*
Perilla frutescens, 70
Periwinkle. *See Catharanthus roseus*
Petroselinum crispum, 70
Pimpinella anisum, 71
Pineapple sage. *See Salvia elegans*
Pomegranate. *See Punica granatum*
Poncirus trifoliata, 71
Poppy. *See Papaver rhoeas*
Poterium sanguisorba, 72
Pot-marigold. *See Calendula officinalis*
Potpourris, 30, 119
Prince's-feather. *See Amaranthus hybridus hypochondriacus*
Punica granatum, 72
Pyrethrum. *See Chrysanthemum coccineum*

Quamash. *See Camasia esculenta*

Rheum rhabarberum, 73
Rhubarb. *See Rheum rhabarberum*
Roman chamomile. *See Chamaemelum nobile*
Rosa gallica officinalis, 73
Rose. *See Rosa gallica officinalis*
Rosemary. *See Rosmarinus officinalis*
Rose-scented geranium. *See*

   Pelargonium graveolens
Rosmarinus officinalis, 74
Rue. *See Ruta graveolens*
Rumex scutatus, 74
Ruta graveolens, 75

Safflower. *See Carthamus tinctorius*
Saffron. *See Crocus sativus*
Sage. *See Salvia elegans; Salvia officinalis*

Salad burnet. *See Poterium sanguisorba*
Salvia elegans, 75
Salvia officinalis, 76
Santolina. *See Santolina chamaecyparissus*
Santolina chamaecyparissus, 76
Satureja hortensis, 77
Satureja montana, 77
Savory. *See Satureja hortensis; Satureja montana*
Scarlet bee-balm. *See Monarda didyma*
Seeds, growing from, 13-19, 109
Sesame. *See Sesamum indicum*
Sesamum indicum, 78
Shade, herbs for, 112
Shirley poppy. *See Papaver rhoeas*
Soil preparation, 25
Sorrel. *See Rumex scutatus*
Spearmint. *See Mentha spicata*
Spices, herbs compared with, 9
Stachys byzantina, 78
Stachys olympia, 78
Summer savory. *See Satureja hortensis*
Sun, herbs for, 111
Sweet basil. *See Ocimum basilicum*
Sweet bay. *See Laurus nobilis*
Sweet Cicely. *See Myrrhis odorata*
Sweet heliotrope. *See Heliotropium arborescens*
Sweet marjoram. *See Origanum majorana*
Sweet violet. *See Viola odorata*
Sweet woodruff. *See Galium odoratum*
Symphytum officinale, 79

Tagetes erecta, 79
Tanacetum vulgare, 80
Tansy. *See Tanacetum vulgare*
Tarragon. *See Artemisia dracunculus sativa*
Tea, herbs for, 28, 116
Teasel. *See Dipsacus sylvestris*

Terraced herb garden, 94–95
Teucrium chamaedrys, 80
Thyme. *See Thymus vulgaris*
Thymus vulgaris, 81
Top onion. *See Allium cepa proliferum*
Trigonella foenum-graecum, 81
Tropaeolum majus, 82
True chamomile. *See Chamaemelum nobile*
True lavender. *See Lavandula angustifolia*

Valerian. *See Valeriana officinalis*
Valeriana officinalis, 82
Vegetables, herbs compared with, 9
Verbena. *See Aloysia triphylla*
Vinca. *See Catharanthus roseus*
Vinegars, 28, 119
Viola odorata, 83
Violet. *See Viola odorata*

Watercress. *See Nasturtium officinale*
Welsh onion. *See Allium fistulosum*
White horehound. *See Marrubium vulgare*
Wild indigo. *See Baptisia australis*
Wild marjoram. *See Origanum vulgare*
Winter savory. *See Satureja montana*
Woodruff. *See Galium odoratum*
Wooly betony. *See Stachys byzantina*
Wormwood. *See Artemisia absinthium*

Yarrow. *See Achillea filipendulina*

Zingiber officinale, 83